THE MEDITATION RETREAT MANUAL

THE MEDITATION RETREAT MANUAL
In Search of Ultimate Peace

By
Peter Stuckings

AEON

First published in 2023 by
Aeon Books

Copyright © 2023 by Peter Stuckings

The right of Peter Stuckings to be identified as the author of this work has been asserted in accordance with §§ 77 and 78 of the Copyright Design and Patents Act 1988.

All rights reserved. No part of this publication may be reproduced, stored in a retrieval system, or transmitted, in any form or by any means, electronic, mechanical, photocopying, recording, or otherwise, without the prior written permission of the publisher.

British Library Cataloguing in Publication Data

A C.I.P. for this book is available from the British Library

ISBN-13: 978-1-80152-093-5

Typeset by Medlar Publishing Solutions Pvt Ltd, India

www.aeonbooks.co.uk

*Dedicated to all meditators everywhere.
May you find ultimate peace in this very life.*

CONTENTS

INTRODUCTION   xi

PART I: RETREATS: PHYSICAL

CHAPTER ONE
Meditation equipment   3

CHAPTER TWO
Noble Silence   7

CHAPTER THREE
Meals   11

CHAPTER FOUR
To bring or not to bring   15

CHAPTER FIVE
Journaling   19

CHAPTER SIX
Pali chanting and formalities   23

CHAPTER SEVEN
Finding a centre   29

CHAPTER EIGHT
Discomforts and inconveniences   35

CHAPTER NINE
Ordination on retreat   41

CHAPTER TEN
Donations   45

CHAPTER ELEVEN
Visas and international travel   49

CHAPTER TWELVE
A day on retreat   53

INTERLUDE 1
Concentration meditation instructions   59

PART II: RETREATS: MENTAL

CHAPTER THIRTEEN
Preparing yourself   65

CHAPTER FOURTEEN
Commitment vs. Quitting   69

CHAPTER FIFTEEN
Devices   73

CHAPTER SIXTEEN
East and West   77

CHAPTER SEVENTEEN
Teachers   85

CONTENTS   ix

CHAPTER EIGHTEEN
Continuity of practice   89

CHAPTER NINETEEN
Sleep time   93

CHAPTER TWENTY
Mental health   95

CHAPTER TWENTY-ONE
Other meditators   101

CHAPTER TWENTY-TWO
Leaving retreat   105

INTERLUDE 2
Insight meditation instructions   107

PART III: MEDITATION: PHYSICAL

CHAPTER TWENTY-THREE
Morality   113

CHAPTER TWENTY-FOUR
Aches and pains   117

CHAPTER TWENTY-FIVE
Postures   123

CHAPTER TWENTY-SIX
Samatha vs. Vipassana   133

CHAPTER TWENTY-SEVEN
Restraint of the senses   139

CHAPTER TWENTY-EIGHT
Anicca   143

CHAPTER TWENTY-NINE
The meditation hall   149

CHAPTER THIRTY
Exercising 151

CHAPTER THIRTY-ONE
Daily practice post-retreat 153

INTERLUDE 3
Walking meditation instructions 157

PART IV: MEDITATION: MENTAL

CHAPTER THIRTY-TWO
Effort 161

CHAPTER THIRTY-THREE
The Five Hindrances 165

CHAPTER THIRTY-FOUR
Maps 171

CHAPTER THIRTY-FIVE
Faith 177

CHAPTER THIRTY-SIX
Mindfulness vs. Concentration 181

CHAPTER THIRTY-SEVEN
Conceit 183

CHAPTER THIRTY-EIGHT
Enlightenment 187

CHAPTER THIRTY-NINE
Dark Night 197

FURTHER RESOURCES 203

ABOUT THE AUTHOR 207

INDEX 209

INTRODUCTION

Sign at the Buddha's birthplace, Lumbini, Nepal

It is no exaggeration that the path of intensive meditation training may turn out to be the most illuminating and rewarding journey of your life. I hope you stick around long enough to see this for yourself because the reasons are not immediately apparent.

From the outside, it makes little sense why people go to a remote place to sit in silence hour after hour, for many days or even months in a row. It would be easy to conclude retreats are all about mystical mumbo jumbo or avoidance of life challenges. In fact, meditation is not a state of shutting down or doing nothing. Despite how static it might appear, meditation actually involves navigating a path of developmental changes. You could think of it as a complex journey to the heart of the human condition. At times exhilarating, at times painful, the journey is ultimately profoundly rewarding. And along the way there are fascinating landscapes, evolving perspectives, and an eventual destination of sorts.

The landmarks on this journey can be mind-blowing, mind-numbing, heavenly, disturbing, transformative, and more. But—and here is the point of this book—you must walk it for yourself. The discoveries cannot be explained in words that replicate the experience. If someone were to try, the uninitiated would link up those words with old familiar concepts and settle for an understanding that falls short. Meditation shows us precisely that which is obscured from our normal untrained view, so it must be experienced to become known.

If meditation only showed us conditions available in normal daily life, there would be little of interest in it. But with enough practice at what we call purifying the mind, one can arrive at states of peace, stillness, and release that have no comparison in one's life prior to taking up meditation. These experiences can leave us breathless and astonished to discover there is so much more to be felt and known throughout this body-mind complex than we could have imagined. And eventually we may see the greatest of benefits unfold: the overflow of meditation learnings into our daily lives such that we begin to walk a different, more aware path. Again, this is why each of us must undergo the training in order for the fruits to be revealed and lived.

As you might guess, getting to grips with all that one can encounter in the world of meditation training is no walk in the park. And yet the greatest of hindrances we will face are the ingrained habits of mind that we ourselves bring to the task. I'm reminded of the old Zen trope of the teacher standing before his students guiding them to see the brilliance of the moon. But instead of observing the moon, the students are fixated on his pointing finger. You can imagine the teacher's struggle. "There it is," he says, gesturing. "Yes, we see," they reply, nodding at the finger. "No, not that," the teacher counters. He points more emphatically. "*There!*" "Yes, we understand," the students nod again.

If we are satisfied we know something, the mind has effectively closed the door on the matter, convinced it has no need to search any further. But if what we have settled on is wrong or incomplete, it's an uphill battle to update that understanding. Such is the perennial problem we face when approaching the Buddha's discoveries about the mind. We are setting out to investigate that which has always been right before our eyes, but has routinely escaped notice. So it serves us well to bring to meditation what the Zen Buddhists call beginner's mind: the approach of assuming nothing and being open to learn anew in every moment. Because understanding is always a work in progress, not a static destination point.

* * *

In this book you will find advice on the questions people come upon when starting out in the practice of intensive meditation. Everything from basics like what to bring on a retreat and how to sit well, to the mental and conceptual challenges commonly faced. It's less of a narrative from start to end and more of a reference text, so feel free to skip to the topics you're interested in.

There are some meditation instructions throughout the book to pique your interest, and recommended information sources in the Further Resources section at the rear. To ensure everyone is on board, I start with the basics and encourage you to find out what's next. And finally, there is a focus on meditation methods with roots in the Buddhist teachings.

Diverse "Buddhisms" abound everywhere from Japan to Sri Lanka and from Tibet to Taiwan, not to mention the offshoots that have taken root elsewhere around the world. The major Buddhist strands are as follows. Note that each of these consists of sub-strands.

- Theravada (South and South-East Asia): the term means Word of the Elders, referring to the tradition's aim to adhere to the earliest extant texts, and features a focus on individual liberation through asceticism and meditation.
- Mahayana (East and North-East Asia): the term means Big Vehicle, and is a later development marked by philosophical investigation, religious observances, and a shift away from individual salvation to a society-wide project of saving all beings.
- Tibetan (or Vajrayana) (Tibetan plateau and northern India): a complex collision between Mahayana strands from India and China with pre-existing indigenous beliefs, marked by philosophical investigation and innovative rituals and meditation techniques.

The main meditation methods you may encounter are as follows, but this list is not exhaustive.

- Vipassana: persistently observing mental and physical phenomena until intuitive insights arise. Traditionally considered part of Samatha, but in the modern age it is increasingly taught as a separate training.
- Samatha: a range of concentration practices that investigate mental and physical states.
- Vajrayana/Tantra: esoteric practices such as mantras and visualisations. Includes Dzogchen techniques of observing the ground of consciousness.
- Zen: a Japanese term derived from the Sanskrit word *dhyāna* meaning meditation, appearing also in Chinese as Chan, in Korean as Son, and in Vietnamese as Thien. The meditation is mostly derived from Samatha with some added East Asian characteristics.
- Combinations, variations, and modern bootlegs of these.

The one feature common to all of these meditation methods is that each one is the only pure, true way to Enlightenment as intended by the Buddha. All the others are inferior corruptions. If you don't believe me, just ask an adherent of each one!

Jokes aside, it helps to be on our guard against attachment to traditions and methods. Long-term meditation practice eventually reveals the basic truth that the mind more or less instinctively knows the way to the ultimate peace. It just needs the opportunity to get there, much like a wild animal in a cage only needs the latch lifted to make good its escape. So it's less important which tradition you start with and more that you diligently do the practice until the way forward is revealed. And of course, we should not shy away from learning what each method has to offer. In the meantime, it is all too easy to get caught up in attachment, analysis, and even argumentation. As you become more familiar with the methods, you will see their underlying assumptions as well as their likely benefits and outcomes, not to mention your own deeper motivations. Then you will be better positioned to choose where to focus your energies.

Anyway, no matter the tradition, meditation retreats tend to share the same basic formula: we remove ourselves from the busy world to a quiet place where we commit to a daily routine of meditation training.

There may also be further activities such as a daily lecture, a teacher interview, or a chanting session.

The practice of retreating harks back to the dedicated training undertaken by monks and nuns in the Buddha's time of the fifth to sixth century BCE. In those days it was common for monastics to strive for intensive meditation training in their daily routines, but it was not always possible. They had chores and duties, as well as a need to keep on the move between kingdoms, districts, and towns in order not to exhaust the patronage and patience of the communities they depended on for food and other material support.

As it turned out, every year they got the chance for focused, committed training. A custom among ascetics at the time was to stay put during the three-month rainy season that usually falls between July and October across northern India, due to the difficulty of travel as well as the danger of damage to budding crops. The Buddha made this sedentary period into a formal custom for the growing population of monastics who followed him. The Pali term for rain, *Vassa* (Sanskrit: *Varṣa*), is still used today for the Rains Retreat, the three-month period when monastics are expected to settle down for meditation and study.

During the *Vassa*, the Buddha's monastic population took up a daily routine of rising early, gathering food donations from nearby communities, and spending the remainder of the day and night in meditation practice. Sometimes a senior teacher, possibly even the Buddha himself, would deliver a lecture to help clarify a technical point or to inspire the trainees with a discourse on the benefits of the practice.

Throughout the twenty-five centuries-long history of Buddhist meditative practices, some lay people also wanted to train seriously in these methods. They typically had to fit the practice into their daily household routines which, if you've ever tried it, is a challenge even for us modern folks with time-saving luxuries like washing machines and microwave ovens.

While dedicated meditation practice among lay people was fairly rare until modern times—that's what the monastic life was for—it grew quickly in the twentieth century in the wake of European colonial upheavals across Asia in the nineteenth century. One obvious example is the changes in Burma. The newly arrived colonial authorities removed the monarchy and thereby cut off the traditional imperial protection of and financial support for monasteries. The monks were forced to turn to the civilian population which, by the twentieth century, gave rise to a new relationship of interdependence and cooperation. Through regular contact with the community, meditation masters discovered there were many among the population who wished to strive for the highest goals of the practice, previously available only to monks and nuns within the monastic institutions. In the mid-twentieth century, some Asian teachers even began going abroad to teach, while students from around the world travelled to Asia to train.

Throughout these changing times, it is also true that Buddhist meditation methods and their theoretical frameworks have evolved to suit a more lay-oriented mass market. You may hear teachers and schools claiming their method is exactly the way the Buddha taught his followers to meditate. Too much time has passed and too much interpretation has been added to the remnants of his earliest teachings for this to be entirely knowable. Hence, this is why among the world's meditators is a subset of people seeking out the most reliably effective teaching and training approaches and, as you might expect, these are rarely found in mainstream meditation settings.

Nowadays there are countless meditation retreat centres in most Asian countries, and centres have also proliferated elsewhere around the world. As a result, taking time out to go train at a meditation retreat is now within the reach of unprecedented numbers of people. There are no formal limits to who can attend, and these days people of every age and stage of life, and every cultural and religious background are giving it a try.

Around the world, people are discovering that retreats allow for greater intensity of practice. You don't need to prepare meals or go to work, or look after kids or cars or gardens or pets. There may be a few simple chores to perform, but generally you need only concern yourself with joining the training sessions on time. This ensures you get plenty of consistent, uninterrupted meditation time out of each day. A well-run meditation centre can support a schedule of ten to fourteen or more hours of formal training per day. By comparison, most people in the beginning stages of their daily meditation practice at home may find an hour per day a lot to fit in. Add to this the supportive and cooperative environment of a centre where everyone is tacitly sharing the struggles and joys of the journey together, and you can see how a retreat provides us with unparalleled conditions for strong and intensive practice.

For the record, this is not to suggest there is no benefit to keeping up a basic daily practice over long periods. There certainly is. Meditation is all about developing wholesome habits, including persistent effort, so every little bit counts.

People go on retreats for a range of reasons. Some say it is to better understand the mind or themselves. Others go to training in response to a challenging stage in life. Still others are seeking the highest soteriological goals of the traditional meditation pathways. And it's reasonable that some are responding to all of these.

The word retreat is usually taken to mean withdraw, especially from something difficult or dangerous. But according to dictionaries, it can also mean to go to a quiet, safe place. Or to step back from a position of believing something. Or to remove oneself from the busy world to engage in meditative contemplation. I like to think of going on a meditation retreat as engaging with all of these possibilities.

But we should not entertain any illusions that retreats are a breeze. While some meditation retreat centres are luxurious and comfortable—mainly in Western countries—this is not the norm in the traditional Asian settings where monasteries and meditation centres are generally built and maintained with donations, so they may feature basic structures, simple food, and rudimentary facilities. Add to this the fact that you will be required to practice meditation for all the waking hours when you are not eating or doing daily ablutions, separated completely from your typical daily life habits and comforts, and you can see that a degree of adjustment is required.

You might question why traditional retreats are so austere, or even severe in such places as the forest monasteries of South-East Asia. And certainly, by the standards of modern life, it can be a significant challenge. But the reasons are logical enough. Our daily lives in society are overloaded with mental distractions and addictive attachments, as well as stresses and responsibilities, that churn up the mind like a muddy river. Conversely, intensive meditation practice involves settling the mind until it becomes as still and transparent as a crystal-clear pond. So minimising distractions through simple living conditions is central to the whole undertaking.

Even with supportive training conditions, we will quickly discover there's something especially awkward about sitting in silent stillness for hours. The world's quietest place is said to be a sound-proofed room owned by Microsoft in Redmond, Washington, USA, where the walls absorb all sound, deflecting nothing back to people in the space. Researchers have found the total absence of auditory input means *you* become the sound: your heartbeat, lungs, even the pumping of blood. This removal of external stimuli, and the new focus on our own internal existence, causes such intense discomfort and disorientation that very few people can stay in the room for long. There's an important insight here. Stillness and silence stand in stark contrast to the external noise and disruption that dominate our daily lives, in which we are absorbed in the pursuit of endless entertainments, frivolous distractions, perpetual pleasure-seeking, and fraught displeasure-avoidance. That is, we routinely do everything possible to avoid dwelling in the profound, still, silent awareness of each moment of experience, *as it really is*. The source of this avoidance will likely be revealed on your meditation journey and is one of the most important discoveries we can make about what drives us.

While on retreat, we take advantage of the quiet and solitude to purify the mind. That is, to cleanse it of impurities like anger and lust, stress and worry, and daydreaming and extraneous ruminations. With increased purity, we can cultivate mental skills like concentration and mindfulness, which lead to deep silence, inner peace, and eventually contentment. These wondrous achievements are the foundations upon which the highest of wholesome mental habits can grow: compassion, lovingkindness, joy for the happiness of others, and equanimity. The fruits of meditation training are certainly magnificent and worthy of great effort, but the catch is that there are no shortcuts and no easy ways out.

Although meditation is all about investigating the mind, the mind itself is the most elusive and confounding object of awareness. No matter how hard we try, everything about it seems to evade close examination and comprehension, and all we are left with is questions. What and where and why is the mind? Is it even a thing? To what extent is the mind a transparent representation of the world outside of my experience or to what extent is my experience a figment of the mind's machinations? And is it *my* experience or is there just experience? The more we think about it, the less it seems to make sense.

The good news is that the path of meditation training equips us with the tools of observation as well as concepts and terminology with which to study and discuss what we encounter. I like to think of meditation as a form of empirical investigation. The cushion is my laboratory, concentration my microscope, and mindfulness is there for observing and measuring.

Through mind training we can access heights of mastery unknown prior to setting out. Just as when we witness the greatest feats of sporting mastery—Simone Biles doing flawless backflips across a gym floor or Roger Federer's lightning-fast reflexes on the tennis court—we might marvel at the astounding outcomes of their many years of intensive training. But we should also reflect on the mastery and excellence possible if we approach mind training with the same energy and determination. The mind has significant advantages over the body: it is not subject to the constraints of gravity, inertia, wind resistance, friction, or energy scarcity. The mind has no boundaries, it requires no equipment, it is rooted nowhere, it cannot be boxed in or reduced in any way, and it cannot run out of space or time. Admittedly, the brain is physical, with certain structural and functional characteristics. But it is in no way clear to the observer how the brain gives rise to the compelling and complex universe of consciousness that we typically call the mind.

Having said all of that, meditation training reveals to us that there is one big repository of limitations on mental excellence: ourselves. That is, our inhibitions, preconceptions, and unwholesome thoughts. The good news is they are within our reach to influence.

Such intensive mental training was part of the culture of ancient India. The practice pathways and their goals were predicated on the notion that the mind could be trained, could be manipulated—or, more to the point, unmanipulated—could learn new abilities, could be strengthened along certain performance axes, and could go beyond what untrained people assumed were the bounds of the possible, to arrive at a liberated state of one kind or another. Versions of such training are also available today and are best tackled through the intensive retreat format. Regardless of the claims you encounter on the internet, the same progress is not normally possible when staying at home and listening to apps or learning from books. This is especially true for new starters who can benefit enormously from structured practice and personalised input to get a grounding in the discipline and technique.

In contrast to what the ancients knew, nowadays there's an assumption about the mind that conceals an unhelpful blind spot. We know that physical health requires physical fitness: to be healthy we need to train the body with activities like jogging or cycling or weights. But when it comes to the mind, our culture works on a tacit assumption that everyone starts from a position of mental health and only succumbs to mental illness in unusual or unlucky circumstances. This is a costly misunderstanding.

The mind, no differently to the body, needs training to become and remain strong and resilient. This might be a little confusing at first. The mind isn't really a thing, like a muscle. And it's not a physical organ, like the heart. Instead, you could think of the mind as a stream of processes, or as a conglomeration of instincts and habits that are constantly in flux. It turns out we can neglect these processes and habits and see a decline in our mental capabilities and well-being. Just as we might spend a lot of time on the sofa and then find our bodies unable to cope with the stress of running for a bus, we can also spend our time wallowing in bad mental habits that weaken our clarity and resolve, and leave us more susceptible to unwise or ineffective responses to challenges. So training the mind can help us develop new habits built on strong foundations.

The Buddhist teachings and training methods also show us the mind is the generator of our moment-to-moment experience of reality. It takes sensory data and spins up a heavily processed virtual reality that completely absorbs our attention. We see ourselves as a person with fixed, unchanging attributes embedded in a place and time, engaged in the self-importance of pursuing conceptual desires, and constrained within a narrow perspective of our place in the world as it appears to us. We experience an unshakeable conviction there is a me here and a you there, and a world of things and people around us. Conceptual relationships arise that we invest ourselves in as if they are absolute truths. And as long as we take those concepts to be truths, they become the rationale for our confident engagements with others and the world. The implication of all of this is that our beliefs, which arise out of nothing more than concepts, can embroil us in all kinds of real-world trouble.

And yet—here comes the spoiler!—all of it is illusory. We spend our entire existence embedded so deeply in this thoroughly convincing machinery that we do not think to investigate how authentic our apparent "reality" really is. Driven forth into the world by these illusory perceptions, we may become delusional and act on anger, hatred, lust, jealousy, confusion, dejection, depression, and many other unhappy possibilities that can spread like an infection to those we come into contact with.

In saying our apparent reality is an illusion, I'm not claiming the world of rocks and trees and people does not exist. The issue is that our experience of the world consists of conceptual constructs and deeply flawed assumptions that serve as an overlay on the raw perceptions, obscuring and distorting them to the extent that we no longer experience reality, but instead our mental constructs of it.

Through intensive meditation's heightened awareness of the microscopic activities of the mind, we begin to see this reality construction happening in real time. After seeing through these cognitive processes, new habits arise and we become aware of a clearer and less mediated version of being present in each moment. Tradition tells us the Buddha found that fully awakening to this state of unfiltered awareness was profoundly liberating. It was also irreversible because, once an illusion is busted, it cannot be unbusted: that is, you cannot return to holding a conviction that something is real when you have seen it is false. In English we typically call this accomplishment Enlightenment. Tradition suggests that the extraordinary power and value of his discovery were obvious to him because he spent the remainder of his life—a whole forty-five years—devoted to teaching it to all comers.

The matter of Enlightenment in Buddhist meditation is large and warrants its own chapter. While people seek out meditation training for a range of reasons, Enlightenment (or awakening or other ill-defined spiritual attainments) is a major and important one. We will look at it in detail later.

On a related note, the project of meditation is sometimes misunderstood in the West. It is approached with the self-help expectation of alleviating psychological discomfort or distress, or with the goal of becoming better adjusted and more successful by the standards of society. But Buddhist meditation can actually help you see that the psyche doing all that yearning and suffering isn't as substantial or central to your existence as you might think. People going to meditation to "get" something for themselves are missing the point entirely. Instead, there is only the letting go of an illusion of fixed, permanent self-identity. After this liberative realisation, suffering is likely to be experienced in a quite different way.

It must be stressed this book is not about faith-based religion or mystical beliefs. You do not need to buy into any dogmas in order for meditation to work for you. Just turn up, do the training, and you will see for yourself. For the record, I do not consider myself religious, or beholden to one orthodoxy or another. I do not believe in or advocate clinging to a particular tradition or method, and I do what I can to seek only what is wise and beneficial. Admittedly, this is always a work in progress.

One does not need to be religious to recognise that the Buddha's teachings, as we have them, are among the highest watermarks of human wisdom and therefore deserve sincere study. But here's the catch: he taught an experiential path that opens up direct insights, rather than mere philosophical speculations. Hence why *doing* the meditation is central to this entire project. All else is distraction. Sure, theoretical study is helpful, but only to support our practice. If it grows to become more than that, we have put the cart before the horse. Besides, between retreats there is always time to read and learn. It is not necessary to put training aside to do this.

Over the years, I have encountered an explosion of people online and out there on the trail eager to go further but who are beset by questions. After countless emails and conversations with seekers from every part of the globe, I put together this book to address the most common concerns raised, overheard, or anticipated. I also took the opportunity to pepper a few opinions throughout that were gained through personal experience.

The sole aim of this book is to encourage you to overcome your hesitations. If you are uncertain about how to begin or how hard it might be, I have set out to answer those questions and resolve those doubts. If after reading this book you go and complete a meditation retreat, my efforts will have been more than repaid.

A very sincere thank you to the friends who have given immensely helpful feedback. Without your help, this manuscript would have remained lurking in an obscure corner of the internet. Deep gratitude is due to Josep Maria Prat Vilà, Benoit Anand, and David Pandt for their time and thoughtful critiques. While their input was of great benefit, I take full responsibility for the views expressed and mistakes herein.

You'll also find a listing of meditation centres around Asia at my blog, Places To Meditate.

May you find in these pages the inspiration to go in search of ultimate peace.

Peter Stuckings
March 2023
Sri Lanka

PART I

RETREATS: PHYSICAL

To see what is in front of one's nose needs a constant struggle.
—George Orwell, author

CHAPTER ONE

Meditation equipment

We modern folks are surely not as tough as the meditators of ancient times. They had no fancy halls, cushions, fans, or mosquito nets! They were reputed to have sat on tree roots or simply laid a cloth on the ground. And they sat for many hours, in any weather, exposed to insects, wild animals, bandits, and countless other hazards and discomforts. But these days we are thankfully equipped with a range of creature comforts to help us through the challenges of sitting a meditation retreat.

First off, let's get this basic fact out of the way: there's no such thing as a perfect sitting posture. No matter how you sit, sooner or later you will experience discomfort and a desire to change posture. As counterintuitive as it seems, our experience of the body when sitting in meditation is determined by the state of the mind, not by some long-ago injury to our knee or back, or the hardness of the floor, or a feeling of fatigue in the legs. At various stages along the path of meditational development, we will experience a wide range of bodily manifestations: from blissful comfort in a variety of postures, to pain and discomfort even in the most supportive sitting conditions. For example, on day one of a retreat, we may find it painful and tiring to sit still for just twenty minutes. After a week or two of diligent practice, we may experience energetic and comfortable sitting sessions that go on for two hours without a posture change. The best we can do at the outset is to determine which posture allows us the least discomfort so we can make inroads into the practice. Like any other intensive training activity, with time and experience we will become adept at managing the challenges.

To start, we need a mat. In some centres they are thick and padded; in others, thin and barely providing any comfort at all. A few rare meditators like to sit flat on a mat without a further aid. But normally on top of the mat there is the option of:

- A cushion. Including circular, rectangular, half-moon shape, ramp-shaped, inflatable, and cotton-, seed-, or husk-filled. They are all different, so be sure to experiment.

- A bench. This is a wooden seat, usually foldable and sometimes adjustable, that allows for sitting in a kneeling posture.

 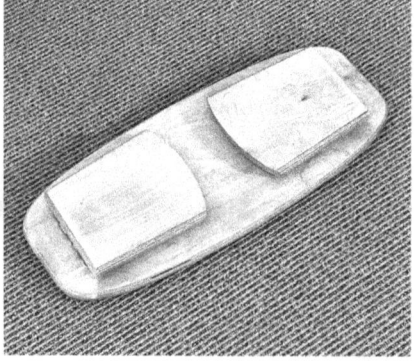

Then there is the humble chair. Increasingly, Western meditators use chairs on retreat, which was frowned upon traditionally. Over the years I've had countless queries about this from Western meditators who insist they'll only go on retreat where they're permitted to use a chair. The good news is these days chairs are generally tolerated by teachers and other meditators alike, wherever you care to go.

In some cases a chair is important, such as for older folks or those with a medical condition. But there is also a growing trend for young, able-bodied meditators to resort to chairs, becoming attached to this mode of sitting, and then using them in all sitting sessions. In the long run, this will not be helpful so it's a good idea to develop the discipline of floor-sitting.

As stated above, one of the most important discoveries we can make on our first retreat is that the painful or pleasant feelings occurring in the body are a result of the state of one's mind and are not simply a matter of what one's sitting posture is doing to a certain part of the body. Of course, some basic physical comforts do make a difference, but the ultimate lesson is that the pain will fade away or become manageable when our concentration and mindfulness are strong. It's important to work on developing a balanced, upright, and well-supported posture so our practice improves to the point where pain is less and less disruptive.

One final item that I recommend taking to a retreat is a shawl or small blanket, climate allowing of course. When you sit still, you may notice the body cools down and you become more sensitive to any cold that might be there, including air conditioning. Bring an extra layer that you can easily put on, take off, or adjust. And let's face it, shawls are undeniably cool!

CHAPTER TWO

Noble Silence

One of the defining features of a meditation retreat is what's known as Noble Silence, a set of rules circumscribing our communication and noise. Each centre enforces and encourages adherence to the rules differently. Some are very strict and quiet, while elsewhere people chat and make noise often.

Most people know Noble Silence means not talking, but it also covers all modes of communication and sources of distraction that our conduct can cause. Which is more important than it may seem. Picture a pond where the water has settled to a glassy, still surface. Then imagine tossing a small pebble into that water and witness how disturbed and churned up it becomes, all from such an insignificant input. Silence fosters a calm and focused mental environment, whereas noise can cause scattering and turmoil. Protecting the retreat setting from unnecessary disruptions is important for everyone's benefit, and that's why Noble Silence requires the participation of each of us.

Since Noble Silence refers to communication of all kinds, it also covers eye contact, hand signals, body language, passing notes, and any other methods you can think of. Once you've committed to the routine of a retreat, it's best not to enter into any kind of interaction with the other meditators. If you have an awkward run-in with another person, you might be left with a lot to think about and no chance to clear it up with them. And don't forget that whatever interaction you have with someone else affects them as well. On a retreat with little to no human contact, such matters can take on a much bigger significance. Best to save the nods or waves or hellos until after the retreat.

Furthermore, these days there's a new form of disturbance the Buddha never had to advise against: mobile device usage. See the section on Devices for warnings about this. A monk once suggested to me we can think of internet use as a form of idle chatter. It similarly fills the mind with distracting trivia with no benefit.

Let's also not forget bodily noises such as burping, sniffling, sneezing, coughing, clearing the throat, and more. Of course, some outbursts of noise such as a sudden cough or sneeze may be unavoidable and are generally easy for others to ignore. But for some folks, the agitation and restlessness they experience during the training can be too difficult to cope with, and they may seek to release the tension through noisy behaviour. You may hear repeated hacking of phlegm or sniffling or grunting or shuffling about on the cushion. One common noise heard on retreat is the big in-breath followed by a loud, sighing out-breath. In the end, we all have to be accommodating and accepting of the struggles of other meditators. But for our own conduct, it's a gift to our fellow meditators when we notice such urges arising and restrain ourselves.

Also note that synthetic textiles such as nylon and ripstop, including puffer jackets, as well as zippers, can make a lot of noise in the quiet environment of a meditation hall. At least one popular meditation centre bans nylon and puffer jackets from the hall.

Whatever measures are in place, sooner or later you are likely to encounter behaviour that is disruptive of everyone's practice. Like the fellow I trained with who had a particular way of noisily wrenching open the door to the meditation hall then slamming it behind him. Every single time.

Here instead is an example of a different kind of behaviour we should all try to cultivate. Imagine you enter the meditation hall early while it's still empty, sit down alone, close your eyes, and go deeply into your practice. At the end of the hour, you open your eyes and are surprised to find all your neighbours sitting in place, quietly meditating. To realise they had entered the room, moved to their places, sat down, and begun their practice, all without a sound, and making that extra effort out of consideration for others, can be a big source of gratitude and loving-kindness towards our fellow retreatants.

Remember:

> *The person you notice least on your retreat may be the most considerate one there.*

Let's all support each other's training by trying to be that inconspicuous person. Here are some tips to help with the practice of Noble Silence:

- Only bring into the hall what you absolutely need in there, which means leaving outside the jacket, notebook, pen, thermos, water bottle, and so on.
- Move slowly and carefully when around others.
- Open and close doors with utmost care, and ask the staff or a teacher first if you want to open or close windows.
- Avoid using noisy time-keepers in the hall such as beeping clocks or watches.
- Be aware of the inadvertent sounds we make such as humming, sniffling, chattering to ourselves, or heavy breathing.
- Do your utmost to be invisible and unobtrusive as this will foster an atmosphere of respectful quietude.

Admittedly it's not possible to avoid communication at all times. Imagine arriving at a doorway at the same time as another person, or at the breakfast buffet. Who should go first? How do I signal to the other person to go? These situations can be easily resolved if one of us steps back and waits for the other to go first. In our interviews with teachers, we can talk as much as we like, which is sometimes a welcome respite and a chance to vent any pent-up feelings. And on long-term retreats, we may want to connect with other meditators when departing, especially if we all leave on different days. So a practice of leaving a note with contact details seems commonly accepted. Just be aware that any communication you initiate with another person who is continuing on after you leave can have repercussions for them.

In the end, if we experience disturbances, noise, and other forms of turmoil, these are good opportunities to develop compassion for and tolerance of our fellow humans. I long ago discovered a neat principle about noise that made it easier to cope with. Since noise generation requires energy, people (and other animals) will only do it for as long as they feel it's necessary, because it makes them tired. An example is the worker on a nearby renovation who is hammering or drilling or sawing. It may seem incredibly disruptive and annoying to us and we worry it'll go on all day. But in fact the worker is getting tired with every strike or stroke and will only keep it up for as long as they have to do it. So that means it'll be over soon, whether in a few seconds, or in a few minutes. Either way, it's not worth getting worked up over, and when the noise is gone, your continuously calm mind will return to the practice all the more quickly for having brought patience and forbearance to the experience.

CHAPTER THREE

Meals

Along with sleep, this is the biggest source of questions. Yes, it's true that the standard on meditation retreats is breakfast and lunch only, both served before midday. But no, it's not true that this is difficult to endure.

All the way back to the Buddha's time in the sixth century BCE, people training under his guidance were obliged to do their eating before midday. The routine for monks and nuns, who typically collected donations of food in the morning, was to eat till satisfied in one or two sittings, and go on with the rest of their daily and nightly routine without eating again. The reasoning is simple: a digestive system that is churning away processing food draws energy and focus away from other activities. You must have noticed how drowsy you feel after a large meal. Therefore, to support an energetic mind, it is best to eat all you need in a limited period in the morning, and devote the rest of the day and evening to the training. It really does help.

Further to this, the Buddha also included a rule about individuals not storing food. All leftover food not consumed was to be discarded when the morning's eating was over. This was probably to ensure monks maintained interdependence with the community, and it surely also had to do with the lack of storage options: there was no refrigeration or airtight containers. Food would have quickly gone off, attracted wildlife, or been overrun with insects. So in the interests of food safety, eating was to be done in a short period and all leftovers promptly thrown away.

A meditator's adjustment to the two-meals-a-day routine should be quick. Within a few days of beginning the retreat, you will notice you are used to the eating times and feel light and free of drowsiness later in the day. You might start out unsure, but you will eventually be surprised how good you feel.

On the bright side, it's not as absolute a limit as it sounds. Centres, traditions, and countries differ on what's acceptable after midday. One might say water only, another says any liquid is fine including coffee and milk, and for yet others, fruits or sweets are fine.

While Buddhist cultures tend to be aware of vegetarianism and are often vegetarian-friendly, it is not always the case. In some Buddhist settings, meat is very much the standard. If you are vegetarian or vegan, it's best to let the centre know in advance as they can usually cater to your needs if they know. In Asia, vegetarian roughly means vegan because dairy is not normally used in cooking and eggs are usually avoided because of the (incorrect) assumption that a chicken's egg contains a foetus and is therefore like meat. But veganism—avoiding consumption of anything in the production of which an animal was used—is a new idea in some cultural settings. If you're vegan, like me, and heading to a foreign country for a retreat, my advice is to adopt a flexible attitude. There are few clearer signs of a meditator's conceit and insensitivity than to arrive in a new place and begin instructing people on what's right and wrong. Sure, some day those values we hold dear may become global and universal, but for now they're not. It is not at all a given in most Buddhist cultures that one must be vegetarian or even be sensitive to these matters. That is one of the many Western projections onto Buddhism.

Some people are sensitive to spicy food and this can be a concern in various parts of Asia, so it's best to check on arrival. Major monasteries in South-East Asia usually offer non-spicy alternatives for foreign meditators.

On the topic of body fuel, be wary of giving in to the need for caffeine, at any time of the day. It might be the magic booster that gets you through a tough day of work or study, but in meditation training we never benefit from a mind racing with an overload of activity, or energetic peaks and sleepy troughs. For more than a decade before my first retreat, I drank coffee like it was water, chugging down several strong cups every single day. And when work took me to remote places, I'd be sure to bring along a plunger and a bag of freshly ground beans. I got so attached to those daily rituals that I assumed I couldn't survive without the stuff. On my first retreat I was upset to discover there was no coffee, which perhaps I should have anticipated. I was anxious about not being able to function without a frequent caffeine boost, but I was determined to push on. As it turned out, I got through the course just fine, drinking tea and juice instead. By the time I returned to daily life, it was clear my old coffee addiction was responsible for a daily routine of giant agitated spikes and dull moody crashes, a self-undermining cycle that fed on itself. As a result of this insight, the urge to drink a strong coffee never arose again. Now my days are consistently balanced and energetic without any need for such stimulants, and my sleep is also much improved.

The teachings speak of dispassion and renunciation arising naturally as a consequence of seeing the harm we do to ourselves through our addictions, and also due to experiencing the joy of a trained, alert mind. It's like looking down and discovering you're holding a red-hot coal in your hand. Naturally you would drop it with great urgency and there's no way you'd pick it up again. Seeing the harm an addiction does to us works just like this. No conscious, effortful quitting is required.

A retreat affords us these rare chances to have a complete break from our regular consumption habits, so it should be no surprise that through this vacation from routine we discover new, more beneficial ways of living.

One last tip is to leave out the snacks or sweets or other food items you may have decided to take after hearing of the limited eating opportunities. Give the two-meals-a-day routine a try and see how well and clear-minded you feel as the day progresses. When there is no option to eat after lunch and the schedule keeps you occupied, you'll discover it doesn't amount to much of a concern.

For the record, if you are pregnant or diabetic, it's normal for food to be provided later in the day if necessary. Remember that retreat centres are all about setting you up to meditate well, so you are sure to be looked after one way or another.

CHAPTER FOUR

To bring or not to bring

It's time to start sounding like your mother and remind you to pack enough warm clothes. And don't forget your vitamins!

I assume you know the basics of travelling to faraway places, so let's look at what's specific to a retreat environment. A good place to begin is what you shouldn't bring.

As tough as it is to go without distractions, entertainments, and communications for some weeks or months, we should resist the temptation to take things that will end up being an unhelpful hindrance. There are obvious ones like electronic devices, which we'll look at in more detail under Devices. And of course, leave at home anything work- or study-related. You won't be able to get much done and it'll only distract you anyway. The next one is books and other reading material. Again, sheer distraction. The only exception here would be on a long retreat where an appropriate book or two can be inspiring and support your practice. See Further Resources for suggestions.

There are also the less obvious ones. As mentioned in the section on Meals, avoid taking food items. The centre should provide everything you need to stay healthy and energetic throughout your stay. Some people might take a fibre additive, condiments, or vitamins. But stowing in your luggage a supply of cookies, chocolates, or trail mix is not going to be as helpful as you might think. You'll just end up becoming dependent on them, or you'll feel bloated throughout the day when you should feel light and energetic.

Little things you may think are fine to take along but can end up being a hindrance would include mementoes such as photos of loved ones, souvenirs, charms, and the like. These items can trigger memories, thoughts, and inclinations that take us away from what we are at the retreat to train in: staying in the present moment.

And don't forget to leave behind the valuables. If you take jewellery, large amounts of cash, or expensive electronics and then leave them in your room, you can be sure they'll cause worry and distraction. Most centres can lock things away for you if required, but it's wiser to leave them at home.

Then there's clothing. The basic rule for retreats is "conceal don't reveal". For the same reason stated elsewhere in this book, it's really all about distraction. Those images of young men and women in revealing outfits sitting in meditation on a beach while looking blissful and pleased with themselves are about as far from the reality of intensive meditation as can be imagined.

You will find the most suitable clothing is comfortable, loose, and unrestrictive. The climate may be warm, especially if you're in the tropics, and you may have to handwash all these items. So you are best to take light textiles that wash and dry easily. In a cold setting, it's best to take multiple layers that you can remove or put on as the day gets warmer and then gets colder again in the evening. Either way, save the gym outfit and beachwear for when you leave the retreat. In some traditional Asian centres, meditators may be asked to leave if they insist on wearing inappropriate clothing.

While on the issue of clothing, note that in some countries with traditional attitudes to meditation training—mainly Myanmar and Sri Lanka—you are expected to don the local garb, such as the *longyi* (Myanmar) or *sarong* (Sri Lanka). These are long tube skirts for both men and women, often supplied at the meditation centre as well as at local shops. They don't take much to get used to, and they may even help set you up for a more open-minded approach to the meditation practice by taking you out of your normal daily routines and assumptions.

Remember my oft-repeated adage:

> *Your comfort zone is the place where nothing interesting ever happens.*

So don't be shy, give it a try!

On a different note, most centres usually supply some items such as basic linen, although you may prefer to bring your own. Sometimes a towel is supplied, and in some centres a few helpful additions are washing powder, drinking water, and even basic toiletries. But if the centre's communications don't mention such things, best to bring them. In certain locales, especially the tropics, mosquito nets are hung over the beds and also in the meditation hall over your sitting position. Even so, it's always a good idea to bring a supply of insect repellent, because if there's even a single hole in a net, you can be sure a mosquito will find it.

What you should take, beyond the usual clothing and toiletry items, is diverse. Let's take a look at a few. This is not a comprehensive must-have list but just a brainstorm of possible needs.

Standard:

- Insect repellent
- Alarm clock
- Timer such as a wristwatch (your phone may be locked away)
- Basic linen (for single bed)
- Refillable water bottle
- Washing powder for handwashing clothes
- A shawl or light blanket (good for air-conditioned and cool places)
- Basic medications.

Specifically for long retreats:

- Sewing kit (you may want to repair things during your stay)
- Extra toiletries (you'll be surprised how much toothpaste and shampoo you can go through)
- A hair/beard trimmer (you may not want to end up looking like a castaway)
- Extra washing powder
- Compact hair dryer (if you have lots of hair and the climate is humid).

Specifically for Asian settings:

- Power socket adaptors
- Spoon, especially in places where eating with the hands is customary and cutlery may not be supplied

- Even more and different types of insect repellent!
- Flashlight or lamp (it's a fact of some places, especially remote monasteries, that electricity may not be available 24/7).

And finally, optional extras that I tend to recommend:

- Meditation cushion or bench
- Eye mask, for when you find bright light in the meditation space irritating
- Earplugs, for when you want to go deep in your concentration practice, or when there's construction going on right outside, or monastery dogs barking all night
- Soap bars (they're cheap and compact and can last for months).

Again, you needn't worry too much over the details. Retreat centres are committed to accommodating people and helping them meditate well, so they can usually address a wide range of needs. At one centre, for instance, there's a table loaded with every kind of toiletry and pharmaceutical item for meditators to take and use freely. They also have a storeroom packed with spare clothing, shawls, and linen of every description. At some centres there's an electric jug for boiling water in your room. And finally, there's usually a supermarket not far away where you can pick up the basics.

CHAPTER FIVE

Journaling

Should you keep a diary of your meditation experiences while on retreat?

This should be a fairly simple matter but depends on you as well as the meditation tradition. Some people like to keep a daily journal in normal life so the habit would be easy for them to keep up while on retreat. For others it's a painful chore. Also, one major meditation tradition advises against writing while in training. Whereas another major tradition says it's necessary for recording the frequent changes unfolding in your meditation experience.

If you're unsure whether to bother, keep in mind that your experience of the meditation practice will evolve, whatever the tradition, and it can be helpful to record some basic information to follow the history of the developments. Furthermore, some teachers like to conduct detailed interviews, and setting down a summary at least once a day can be a big help.

In my experience, the only hazard is to end up writing too much too often. Any activity that takes us away from diligent continuous practice can grow increasingly attractive during a retreat, especially if we hit any rocky periods on the journey. There's usually at least one person in the meditation hall busily recording their life story in a notebook, scribbling away with an astounding level of energy and dedication for longer than makes sense.

To help get an idea of what's appropriate to record, here's a list of meditation features that a teacher might want to know about.

- Breath: try to note the length, pace, volume, and other measures of the breath. Note for example whether it's calm and relaxed or fast or heavy.
- Posture: look for how it begins, how it changes, and whether aches and pains force you to shift the posture during a sit. Is the back up straight, drooping, leaning, etc?
- Mind: note how your mind seems to be observing experiences. Is it distracted, sharp, clear, energetic, sleepy, slack, spacious, narrow, full of self-referential thoughts or big spiritual ponderings, and so on. Record whether the mind seems deeply interested in the breath or is easily distracted by sounds outside, etc.
- Energy: it's good to note down whether you feel energetic, sleepy, whether the time seemed to race by or drag painfully. Did you find yourself wanting to sit longer or was it a chore to see through the full hour?
- Changes: all of the above will change, sometimes frequently, and so much that it's difficult to record how a feature was at any given moment because of how much it changed. If this is the case, record the sequence of changes the best you can remember. Alternatively, if things don't seem to change much, that's also an interesting contrast that is worth recording.

That's an overview of what you should write about. Consider the following example of an entry I might make at the end of a three-hour morning session.

> 3 Jan. morning: at the start, mind was busy, thinking a lot, heartbeat was fast & heavy, breath was medium length with some mild stiffness, felt moderate energy. Posture was straight up, no shifts till near end of 1st hour. Breath became longer & smoother, eventually fading away till barely noticeable. Mind became clear and quiet. Walked 1 hour, lots mind wandering & daydreaming, struggled to stay present. Back on the cushion, felt tired & lethargic, made lots of

effort to watch the breath, mind occasionally drifting to challenging thoughts including theme of doubting, posture sometimes leaned to the right as if body was tired.

You'll notice this entry only records meditation experiences: no external or extraneous matters such as what other people were doing or what the weather was like. This is what teachers are usually looking for. That is, how the breath, body, and mind are manifesting in your awareness throughout the day. Importantly, notice I haven't detailed what the thinking was about, only that there was thinking and that it was persistent, unpleasant, or the like. Some people can get deeply entangled in recording the content of their thinking, writing up a storm about their memories of past hurts, misdeeds, wrongs they've suffered, hopes for the future, plans for after the retreat, and so on. It can be never-ending. This kind of self-absorbed self-analysis is closer to psychotherapy, which is a perfectly reasonable process to undergo, except it's not what we go on retreat for.

A focus on content will lead to time wasted on what is basically just the mind's business of keeping active with self-defending histories and concerns about an unknowable future. If you feel the content that is coming up is powerfully important and is revealing all the causes of unhappiness in your life, then that sounds promising. But it's likely to be just another distraction orchestrated by a restless mind. An effective strategy is to note down these themes in brief bullet points at the back of your notebook for consideration *after the retreat*, and then drop them and get on with the practice. They will eventually pass as these sometimes obsessive themes are just stuff the mind throws up at various stages along the journey of a retreat. Don't get bogged down in them. Alternatively, if those themes feel very important to you, consider going to psychotherapy instead of intensive meditation. Despite the modern Western fascination for mindfulness in healthcare settings, the two processes—meditation and psychotherapy—really are different and operate on different assumptions and levels. They may support each other in the bigger picture of your life, but it's best not to conflate them when on retreat.

In summary, you should keep at least a basic journal throughout your retreat so you can look back and understand the progress that took place, and to report to the teacher should they wish to know the details.

CHAPTER SIX

Pali chanting and formalities

Pali is the language used to memorise and pass down the speeches the Buddha is reputed to have made during his forty-five-year teaching career in the fifth to sixth century BCE. While there is no evidence he actually spoke this ancient Indian language and probably instead taught in a number of regional dialects, Pali has been used to transmit his teachings for well over 2,000 years.

After several centuries of oral transmission, the teachings were set down in writing in Sri Lanka in the first century BCE. Today the modern translations of those texts amount to thousands of pages of hardcover editions. It is mind-boggling to consider the effort by many generations of monks and nuns to memorise, chant, and pass on those teachings. Then there were the many centuries of copying them out by hand in numerous languages across the Eurasian continent to ensure their survival into the age of modern mass printing processes and online sharing. These facts alone should be sufficient inspiration to strive to understand what was so valuable in those texts.

Furthermore, Pali has deeply influenced the national languages where it is still used in Buddhist practice and study, such as Sri Lanka, Myanmar, Thailand, Cambodia, and Laos. Add all these factors together and you'll appreciate the deep reverence Buddhists of those countries have for this language and the texts set down in it.

Because of the oral character of Pali literature, it lends itself well to chanting. So a practice of no small importance across the Theravada Buddhist countries of South-East Asia is the daily chanting sessions in monasteries, temples, and meditation centres. This practice is also often found in new meditation centres around the world today. In some places you are expected to join the sessions. In others it's optional.

Some meditators find the chanting a pleasant break from an intensive meditation schedule and they're happy to join in along with the teacher or resident monks or nuns. It's worth giving it a try. There should be a booklet containing the words and a translation so you can read along and keep up. The chants include recitations of some of the key discourses the Buddha gave, which can be handy to become familiar with as they open up new understandings for our meditation practice. And there are chants offering loving-kindness to others and ourselves, revering the Buddha, his teachings, and the monastic community, or seeking protection from harmful influences such as fear or the forces of nature. Also, when practised often enough, you may begin to experience a degree of meditative concentration and calmness during chanting.

Apart from the daily chanting routine, a retreat may begin with initial chants such as to pay homage to and take refuge in the Buddha, his teachings, and the monastic community, as well as to commit to a set of precepts or vows to govern our behaviour while on retreat. The precepts are an important part of the meditation practice of certain traditions and are not merely a ceremonial formality, as meditators are expected to adhere to those rules during the retreat.

First, the basic Five Precepts cover the major moral transgressions, namely killing (or harming), stealing, sexual misconduct, lying, and intoxicants. An expanded version known as the Eight Precepts is often standard at retreat centres, and these add injunctions against eating after midday, wearing ornaments and perfumes, engaging in music, dancing, and singing, and sitting or sleeping on high seats and beds.

Below is the text with English translation for the three main chants you can expect to find in traditional meditation centres. The first one, the Homage to the Buddha, is also a standard chant before any kind of lecture or teaching session. The second, taking refuge in what is known as the Triple Gem, involves committing oneself to the care of the teacher, the teachings, and the monastic community that fosters these. Then the precepts. The Five Precepts are considered normal for daily life for lay Buddhists, whereas the Eight Precepts are especially for a meditation training setting. Therefore, the third precept in the first set only concerns sexual misconduct, whereas in the second set, celibacy is required while in training.

As for pronunciation, we'll keep it simple. Generally, and conveniently, the letters are mostly pronounced as they look to an English speaker. For example, *dutiyampi* is pronounced "doo-tee-yam-pee". The horizontal stroke above a vowel makes it long. For example, *musāvādā* is pronounced "mu-saa-vaa-daa". Double consonants require the pronunciation of each letter, so *kamma* is "kam-ma", not "ka-ma". The only tricky one to look out for is the final letter ṃ on many words, which is pronounced "ng" as in "sing". So *saraṇaṃ* is pronounced "sa-ra-nang".

Finally, as you'll see below, some lines in Pali are chanted three times. This is a custom from the Buddha's time when to say something once was common and might signal a lack of conviction. To repeat it three times underscored the speaker's sincerity or the urgency of the message. For more information, please take a look at Further Resources.

Homage to the Buddha

Namo tassa Bhagavato arahato sammā sambuddhassa (three times)
Homage to the blessed one, the exalted one, the fully self-
  enlightened one.

Refuge in the triple gem

Buddhaṃ saraṇaṃ gacchāmi.
I go to the Buddha for refuge.
Dhammaṃ saraṇaṃ gacchāmi.
I go to the Dhamma for refuge.
Saṅghaṃ saraṇaṃ gacchāmi.
I go to the monastic community for refuge.
Dutiyampi ... (as above for all three)
For the second time ...
Tatiyampi ... (as above for all three)
For the third time ...

The five precepts

Pāṇātipātā veramaṇī sikkhāpadaṃ samādiyāmi.
I undertake the training rule to abstain from killing.
Adinnādānā veramaṇī sikkhāpadaṃ samādiyāmi.
I undertake the training rule to abstain from taking what is not given.
Kāmesu micchācārā veramaṇī sikkhāpadaṃ samādiyāmi.
I undertake the training rule to abstain from sense pleasure misconduct.
Musāvādā veramaṇī sikkhāpadaṃ samādiyāmi.
I undertake the training rule to abstain from false speech.
Surā meraya majja pamādaṭṭhānā veramaṇī sikkhāpadaṃ samādiyāmi.
I undertake the training rule to abstain from using intoxicants that may cause heedlessness.

The eight precepts

Pāṇātipātā veramaṇī sikkhāpadaṃ samādiyāmi.
I undertake the training rule to abstain from killing.
Adinnādānā veramaṇī sikkhāpadaṃ samādiyāmi.
I undertake the training rule to abstain from taking what is not given.
Abrahmacariyā veramaṇī sikkhāpadaṃ samādiyāmi.
I undertake the training rule to abstain from sexual activity.
Musāvādā veramaṇī sikkhāpadaṃ samādiyāmi.
I undertake the training rule to abstain from false speech.
Surā meraya majja pamādaṭṭhānā veramaṇī sikkhāpadaṃ samādiyāmi.
I undertake the training rule to abstain from using intoxicants that may cause heedlessness.
Vikāla bhojanā veramaṇī sikkhāpadaṃ samādiyāmi.
I undertake the training rule to abstain from eating at the wrong time.
Nacca gīta vādita visūkadassana mālāgandha vilepana dhārana maṇḍana vibhūsanaṭṭhānā veramaṇī sikkhāpadaṃ samādiyāmi.
I undertake the training rule to abstain from dancing, singing, music shows, using garlands, perfumes, cosmetics, adornments, and ornaments.
Uccāsayana mahāsayana veramaṇī sikkhāpadaṃ samādiyāmi.
I undertake the training rule to abstain from using high, luxurious seats and beds.

If you wish to take the precepts seriously and should you find yourself breaking any of them, it is customary to ask the teacher to "give" you the precepts again, which simply involves going through the chant again. Most of these rules are not considered to be unbreakable and there is no fixed punishment for failing to adhere to them. Consider them more as guidelines to help you avoid getting into conflicts or difficulties with those around you. Having said that, in the case of sexual misconduct or intoxication, it would be normal for disciplinary action to be taken as these are serious matters.

While Pali is the earliest language in the world of Buddhist texts, you may also encounter Tibetan, classical Chinese, Sanskrit, as well as local languages. In Myanmar, for example, chanting is often done in both Pali and Burmese.

Getting to grips with a range of terms in foreign languages is common in Buddhist meditation, and traditional teachers such as monks are very likely to use those terms frequently, so it helps to get to grips with the main ones.

CHAPTER SEVEN

Finding a centre

When you take time out from your busy life to travel across the world, you will naturally need to settle a bunch of details via bookings. There are flights, hotels, and maybe some time for sightseeing. But meditation centres, especially those in remote corners of Asian countries, are sometimes not the easiest places to find reliable information on, or make arrangements with. The following advice specifically regards arranging a retreat at a meditation centre in Asia, since whatever centres are available in your home country likely have plenty of online resources to help you make up your mind as well as supporting details like social media testimonies of like-minded people. Furthermore, some meditation centres in Asia have perfectly adequate online information and do a fine job of communicating with you about your arrangements. So the following information is intended for the more challenging scenarios.

First, it's worth noting there are two main types of venues out there. One is a meditation centre only, with a daily schedule for meditation sessions and meals, as well as an annual schedule of courses or retreats, and also usually at least one teacher in residence. Such places require advance bookings as you are meant to go there on a prearranged date to stay for a prearranged period. These centres are normally run by a monastery or other religious organisation.

The other type of centre is more like a residential monastery, where meditation is possible or encouraged, but there is no retreat schedule and sometimes no meditation teacher in residence. These centres are great for a break after a long retreat, as you can keep up some hours of daily practice while also catching up on other areas of your life such as light exercise, internet communications, reading or studying, and making arrangements for your next move. They are also great for people further along in their practice who simply want a quiet place to work on whatever method they're currently into.

But it is important not to confuse the two. For someone looking for structured training with a teacher's guidance, the latter type of centre is of no use whatsoever. Such centres can also breed laziness because no one is checking up on you and you may be surrounded by people engaged in activities other than meditation, as is often the case in residential monasteries. What's more, there may be events and regular outside visitors, and even distractions like construction or renovation works. These places are helpful at the right time in your journey, but otherwise are to be avoided.

Among the first type, there are centres that run retreats of fixed duration starting and ending on specific dates, and they tend to be open only for specific training courses, so your arrangements with them would need to be locked in ahead of time. On the other hand, there are centres that are open all year round and you just need to let them know when you're arriving.

If a teacher's guidance is important to you, and it should be in the early stages of your practice when you are seeking to gain a foothold in a new technique, the first question is which method you wish to train in. This narrows the vast field of options considerably. Next, you should seek suggestions about training centres from people who have trained abroad in that method. Reaching out to people or doing some online research can help at this stage. There are countless blogs, forums, and subreddits where people discuss their experiences or share details of where they have trained.

Alternatively, you can start from scratch by diving into the internet and sifting through the available options. Either way, the next question to settle is the country. For example, if you wish to train in the Mahasi method, which originates from Myanmar, and that country is currently mostly cut off for international meditators, you could search for Mahasi meditation centres in other South-East Asian countries such as Thailand, Malaysia, Sri Lanka, and Indonesia. If you wish to train in a Tibetan method, you could search for centres teaching that particular method throughout the world, or look at offerings in and around Dharamsala in northern India where the Dalai Lama and his exiled Tibetan community are based, and where there is a smorgasbord of meditation training options.

But here is where I find things can get complicated. An online search for meditation centres around Asia shows a lot of old websites that may be long out of date. Perhaps they found it a chore to maintain their site shortly after setting it up many years ago, so they let it go. A handy clue is the latest updates page, where there are blog entries or video presentations. If the latest content is more than a few years old, you can bet no one pays attention to the accuracy of information on this website, and it's also possible they no longer monitor the modes of contact listed there.

To confirm the information, I always seek to corroborate it with other sources. For example, check out online maps like Google Maps to see if the centre exists at the address shown. Street view can help too, as well as looking at reviews posted there about the centre. The dates of the reviews can indicate whether the centre has had recent visitors. It may also have a social media presence such as a YouTube channel or Facebook group page, which can show whether it is a currently running concern. Your browser's translate function can come in handy here. Messaging through Facebook is also a good way to get in touch with the people at the centre.

While searching, it's handy to note that naming conventions may not be what you expect. If the country uses a script other than the Roman alphabet, when names are transliterated, they may appear in numerous forms. For instance, the Sri Lankan forest monastery Nissarana Vanaya is typically known by its district name, which is variously spelt Meetirigala, Mitirigala, Mitrigala, Mithirigala, and more. Note that internet searches for each version of the district name might return limited or no information.

One of the most common concerns I hear from people looking for retreats abroad goes like this: "I sent them an email ages ago but have had no reply yet." Note that email addresses left on websites some years ago may be long out of use. Or the people receiving your email do not read English, or they just don't check the inbox often. It's also possible some centres are inundated with random questions as well as spam so they just don't reply. In all such cases, the only way forward is to pick up the phone. Check the time zone, give them a call during daylight hours, and see what you can find out. If you call, it shows you are seriously interested and bookings can usually be resolved this way.

One understandable reason for the lack of responsiveness is that the centre may serve a large cohort of local meditators and as a result its staff have little time for the occasional random foreigner asking unusual questions. So if in doubt, give them a call.

Over the years, as I searched for places to go to for training, an unexpected source of support were blogs by individuals who had travelled to those places previously. They left photos and details and opinions, as well as up-to-date contact details, all of which helped me to decide if it was the place for me. So have a think about leaving similar posts for others when you've returned home. It all adds up to help each other out.

After all your preparations and your travels to get there, it's worth keeping in mind that the place may not be everything the photos or details suggested, or it may be that your enthusiasm to go train caused you to overlook some inconvenient details. Like the squat toilets (they're not so bad). Or the tropical humidity. Or the ancient crumbling facilities. There's a wide range of options out there, some modern and comfortable, and some that are challenging. Whatever the case, a big part of the value of going abroad to train is the change of environment that sets you up for new approaches to the project of mind training. You may be pleasantly surprised at what you find. Or the opposite. But calmly accepting what's there and making the most of it is practising the kind of mental approach that prepares you for the best outcomes. I have found that centres with challenging conditions turned out, in hindsight, to deliver some of the most rewarding training experiences.

One more point is for the people who are on the road without an end-date and are looking to hop from centre to centre. This certainly allows for greater flexibility and the freedom to move on from an unsuitable place to a more suitable one. But it comes with challenges. To leave one centre and travel, sometimes internationally, to the next one, you will need to get online and make travel arrangements, which may not be possible at a dedicated retreat centre. This is where the residential monasteries mentioned above come in handy. You can spend some days or weeks to do research, get in touch with contacts or a mentor, and calmly decide where to go next. Or, as I often do, take some days or weeks to hang out by the sea or in a quiet countryside setting, to make the most of whichever amazing country you're in, while you get your bearings and make plans.

CHAPTER EIGHT

Discomforts and inconveniences

If you're travelling to another country to attend a meditation retreat, you may need to adjust to some entirely new experiences. This applies especially to tropical countries where bugs, humidity, the dilapidation of lodgings, and unusual food might all be part of the deal. A good idea is to investigate the best time of year so as to avoid difficult conditions such as wet or hot seasons. But whatever you do, you probably won't be able to avoid insects and wildlife. It's helpful to see these challenges as part of the journey rather than deal-breakers that keep you from setting out.

The section on Pali language shows that in certain traditions you may be required to commit to a precept not to kill or harm others, and this includes insects and animals. So, as tempting as it may be to swat a mosquito, if you wish to take the training seriously, you'll want to find other ways to deal with these local residents. Some centres equip rooms with a butterfly net for catching and expelling insects that have invaded your space. And mosquito coils may be supplied, which are handy in some outdoor settings, but indoors you could just end up gagging on the smoke. Whatever the case, always take insect repellent, use it liberally, and make use of mosquito nets, which are normally supplied throughout the region.

Please note the concern with mosquitoes is only discomfort and annoyance. Health complications like malaria or dengue are not commonplace where meditation centres are situated. Some Western people believe they are at risk of malaria wherever they go in the tropics and even go so far as to take medication, some varieties of which can affect cognition. This is almost always an overreaction as malaria is rare in all but a few harsh places, which you are not likely to go anywhere near. Check authoritative sources such as the WHO on the presence of malaria where you are headed so as to satisfy yourself it is no problem. I have been to countless tropical places including ones infested with mosquitoes, and they've never been a serious problem thanks to nets and repellent. They also tend to come and go at different times of the day and night, so once you get to know the routine, you can take the appropriate steps.

A meditator once contacted me with a fearful concern he'd had on a retreat: the "lizards" in his room. It turns out he'd been at a meditation centre where the huts were each home to several geckos, which typically sit on the ceiling and mind their own business. These little creatures made him so uncomfortable that he quit the retreat early. Unfortunately for people who don't like them, geckos are very common across South-East Asia and cannot be avoided by just going to another retreat centre. The thing to keep in mind is these skittish little creatures are very shy and gentle, will keep their distance, and are much more afraid of us than we are of them. Besides, they eat mosquitoes so they are kind of on our side.

Due to the hot and damp conditions of the tropics, the centre's buildings may also be crumbling, suffering from damp damage, or in need of renovation. These centres are typically built and maintained with donations and the sponsorship of local groups and individuals, as well as by meditators such as ourselves. As non-profit entities, they rarely have plenty of cash flow for addressing all of the maintenance matters that crop up. So some flexibility on our part can go a long way to keeping our mind on the training rather than on the state of faulty fixtures or a mouldy bathroom wall.

On a related point, you will notice traditional meditation centres are generally drab places, lacking in most creature comforts, decorations, stylish embellishments, and the like. This is all about providing low-cost facilities focused on simplicity, solitude, austerity, and mental quietude. For example, pictures on walls as you might find in a hotel or public building would only take the mind away from the present moment to daydreams about other times and places. It's best to train in an environment free of such distractions and luxuries. So an austere and simple setting for training is actually an advantage.

There's a wide range of centres and standards out there. Some places provide comfortable modern mattresses, fans, fridges, hot running water, and even washing machines. Believe it or not, there is also a centre or two with wi-fi. And at the other end of the scale, the accommodation is simple and ascetic. The room may just be a bare concrete space with a window or two, a single lightbulb overhead, and a bed base with a mat or very thin mattress. Such a room may also bless you with the luxury of a single working electricity socket. And of course the shower and toilet facilities are usually very basic. Despite how it sounds, in my experience, the simpler the conditions, the more focused on meditation practice the community of meditators seems to be. It just requires a lifestyle adjustment at the outset. Our reactions to this adjustment process are also precious opportunities to learn about craving and the suffering it causes in us.

But once in a while, a place delivers an experience in a class of its own. I once spent a period in a remote forest monastery in Sri Lanka. I was assigned a single small hut, known as a *kuti*, set in thick woods not far from a toilet block shared with a number of other *kutis*. On the first day as I went to lunch, alone on a remote forest path, my eyes locked onto a six-foot-long snake only inches from my feet. It raised its head to glance calmly at me, probably chuckled to itself about what the newbie had in store, and slithered on its way. It took some minutes for my heart rate to return to normal.

That night, while visiting the toilet block, my flashlight fell upon a large brown tarantula sitting by the toilet stall. I'd seen the captive and cooked ones in Cambodia before, but to be alone at night with a real, live one was a different matter. I had time to notice it was fuzzy and muscular and looked primed to jump at anything. Was it venomous? Was it lethal? Was there a hospital nearby?! The fear was rising. Without taking my eyes off it and while trying to breathe steadily, I reached for the broom in the corner, hoping to prod my frightful foe towards the back door. As I pushed the broom at it, the tarantula sprang up on its hind legs and showed its fangs and fore legs. From out of nowhere came an odd guttural sound. It must've been me. We then proceeded on a chaotic dance together: it lunging at the broom in a daring show of mortal combat with a much bigger threat, me hopping from foot to foot and yelping while prodding it along, all the way out the door into the dark. I leapt back inside, slammed the door, and hoped it was the last I'd see of my new neighbour. The monks in the nearby *kutis* were probably chuckling themselves to sleep.

The next day, following lunch and feeling confident I'd seen all the wildlife there was—how much more could there be, right?—I returned to my *kuti* for some rest and meditation in the hot midday lull. I crunched through the leaves to the door, kicked off my flip-flops, and settled myself inside. After some minutes, a commotion outside drew me to the window. A bunch of small birds were squawking and leaping around on the ground just where I had walked moments before. It took me a while to see the cause of their excitement. Camouflaged among the brown leaves was a small slender snake, perhaps a foot long but curled up to resemble a leaf, with an out-sized arrow-shaped head, the whole thing perfectly blended with its surroundings. Arranged like that, it would fit neatly in the palm of your hand. I must have stepped right over it. A sign at the office had shown this exact kind of snake, a viper, describing it as venomous and to be avoided. As the birds leapt and shrieked and pecked, the snaked lunged at them with fangs bared before springing back to its original position, probably hoping its camouflage would finally work and the birds would leave. I watched for a while, wondering how I would ever set foot outside again. What if I needed to go to the toilet? And what if his pal the tarantula was over there waiting for another twirl around the dancefloor? I decided to sit back and reflect for a while on the intersection between the Buddhist notion of suffering and being surrounded by deadly venomous creatures. Eventually the birds grew tired and left, and then so did the snake.

As it turned out, the wildlife was not the biggest challenge at the forest monastery. The heat, the humidity, the odd meal times, the long distances between facilities, having to wear long white clothing in an environment that was difficult to stay clean in. It all added up to show me I was not ready for that particular level of challenge, so I quit early and moved on to a more urban centre with concrete paths and attached bathrooms. There the spiders were tiny and harmless.

I don't wish to turn anyone away from travelling to challenging meditation centres. On the one hand, such experiences are actually quite rare because most meditators would not venture out to the hardcore forest monasteries, and the occasional wildlife interaction in most meditation centres is harmless enough. Like watching a monkey or tortoise or peacock amble by. Meditation centres are human-dominated places so the wildlife is generally forced to the fringes. On the other hand, some of the more challenging environments such as forest monasteries can suit people who are on a certain kind of quest to explore their tolerances and limits. So the options across the range have their relevance and value.

Regarding urban areas, I find the main concern is the myriad sources of noise. In some countries, people are so accustomed to busy round-the-clock traffic, raised voices, animal sounds, and construction and industrial noise that they simply don't notice it anymore. Add into the mix the fact that your meditation practice may be going through a demanding stage, and you'll become familiar with such mental states as agitation, frustration, and impatience. Of course, earplugs can go a long way to reducing the impact of such challenges. But it's also part of the meditation journey to come face to face with how our minds struggle with the unpleasant aspects of our experience. To be so aggravated by noise on a retreat that we grow angry at others, our circumstances, or even ourselves, is to miss the opportunity to learn valuable lessons about our own suffering. That's a long way of saying that noise, like the other issues in this chapter, is just another potential source of discomfort to learn from and get used to.

I mention all of these details only to give a sense of the worst-case scenario, so you are less taken aback should you find yourself at that end of the spectrum.

One last point is that in some developing country environments such commonplace requisites as round-the-clock electricity and water supply may turn out to be luxuries. So always travel with a flashlight, keep a bucket filled with water in the bathroom as a standby for flushing and rinsing, and consider that dealing with the challenges of your training setting may be an invaluable part of the meditation journey itself.

And remember:

> *Your comfort zone is the place where nothing interesting ever happens.*

CHAPTER NINE

Ordination on retreat

Some meditators take the step to ordain as a monk or nun while on retreat. It may be something you do to augment your training experience, or it may be that during the retreat you are struck with a strong desire to don the robes and become a member of the Buddha's monastic community, known as the *Sangha*. Of course, there is never any obligation or pressure to do it.

Ordaining as a monk or nun usually means shaving your head, replacing your lay clothes with robes, and committing to a set of rules. These detailed stipulations cover all areas of your life, including meals, living quarters, training, and being instructed by a teacher. You may be expected to bow formally to statues and teachers and senior monks; you may be expected to walk every morning to a street or ceremonial hall to collect your day's food; and you may be expected to live among a group of monastics from the local community as well as from around the world. There's a lot to get used to and it can be challenging.

What are the benefits? This is difficult to answer in brief. For some of us, in the midst of the meditation journey we experience a desire to discard all other aspects of our lives and commit ourselves completely to the training. It usually arises out of the realisation that certain trappings are holding us back from further growth, including old habits learned from family influences, the effects of socialisation, or the thinking instilled by our socio-economic milieu. To leave these matters and influences behind may occur to some meditators as a way to advance further. It may turn out to be a short-term experiment or we may discover it suits us so well we never leave. Ultimately it should support our meditation progress, otherwise it can become a new source of distraction.

In Thailand and Myanmar, it is perfectly acceptable to ordain for as short or as long as you like. For example, you could ordain for a few days during a retreat. In those cultures, it is generally believed that any time spent in robes, no matter how short, is a gain for your spiritual progress.

On the other hand, in Sri Lanka it is considered poor form to ordain with anything less than a lifelong commitment in mind. There is a handful of meditation monasteries that buck this trend and are popular places for foreigners to experience the life in robes. Apart from those exceptions, it is a long and involved process to be ordained in Sri Lanka and is only recommended for the serious.

One more option is to ordain at monasteries and meditation centres in countries outside Asia where Asian lineages have established overseas branches. Most Western countries have such places these days.

Some years ago in Sri Lanka, inspired by the monks and nuns I was training among, I decided to ask for ordination. After some days, a ceremony was held, which involved a number of other monks and a lot of chanting in Pali. Then the last of my hair was shaved off. Three monks accompanied me to the next room where they held up robes to form a makeshift changing room for me to discard the last of my lay clothes. They helped me fasten the lower robe, the upper robe, and the outer robe: the three parts of a Theravada monk's traditional red-orange outfit. Wearing this arrangement well and securely took some practice over the coming days.

After all the fanfare and some weeks had passed, I was bemused by how little there was to do. I slept, ate, meditated, sometimes read the classic texts, attended the occasional evening talk, and mostly just hung around.

Eventually, my monk career took a new turn when the teacher requested I go on *piṇḍapāta* (alms round) each morning. This involved walking barefoot to a nearby village and standing in front of each of a few houses per day to receive donations of food. It turned out I usually received far more than I could eat, and upon my return the excess was shared among the other monks and the monastery staff. At first it was an extremely awkward experience, especially when the donors bowed deeply at my feet, but with time I began to see a deeper meaning.

Much of the life of a monastic is about letting go of self-centred expectations and giving up one's discriminating self to the care of external forces. This includes surviving on the generosity and compassion of strangers each and every day. Seeing it for myself, and being required to live from the donations, taught me a lot about the degree of sacrifice required. It was less about the romantic ideal of escape from society into a remote, individualistic quietude, and more about a symbiotic relationship of sharing and caring between the monastery and the wider community. When lived appropriately, the way of the monastic is to become a lightning rod for compassion, spiritual development, and community well-being. By supporting the monastics, the community nurtures this vital component of their culture and civilisation. The monastics' responsibility is to live their way of life wholeheartedly.

These insights helped me to see that my meditation progress was not simply a personal project but part of a wider, civilisational enterprise of spiritual refinement. Naturally, I felt a stronger drive to meditate and conduct myself appropriately.

Eventually my visa ran out and, because I had not made arrangements for an extension, it was time to disrobe and leave. On the one hand, I was pleased to be able to travel freely again, go where I pleased, and eat whatever I liked. But on the other, I sensed this was only the beginning of a longer training that would have to wait for another day.

Based on my very limited experience, I wouldn't recommend or discourage ordination. It is a deeply personal choice and the motivation must come from inside rather than from external pressures. There are long and solemn traditions of ordination in those countries, so it is not something to take lightly, no matter how short a time you wish to try it out for. At the same time, keep in mind that you cannot anticipate how it feels until you are in the midst of that way of life. It can strengthen one's resolve and devotion to the practice. Or it can have other less helpful outcomes.

It's worth noting that there is no one way to lead the life of a monastic. Some monks and nuns become scholars or meditation teachers or administrators. They may become involved in community service or animal rescue. They may teach about Buddhism or meditation at universities or prisons. Some travel widely or publish books or establish new monasteries. And of course some withdraw to remote places where they focus on developing their meditation practice.

To the best of my knowledge, ordination is also available in the Mahayana Buddhist cultures stemming from China, Korea, Japan, Tibet, and so on. It depends on the individual centre as to who they will ordain. In some countries, it is expected that a prospective monk or nun will spend some months in the monastery before ordaining so the teacher can observe their commitment and suitability before taking them on as a trainee. And in some countries there are age limits.

An added benefit of becoming a monastic is that long-term visas may become available to you, as well as financial support for training-related travel and scholastic studies.

I frequently get questions from Westerners about ordaining in Asian countries. My advice is to be cautious. Take it a step at a time: go to the country, check in at the monastery, and begin a retreat or a period of training. Then look around, talk to other monks or nuns, discuss your thoughts with the teacher, and see what comes of it. It may not work out well to leave your home country to directly ordain at a monastery you found online. The culture shock might be more than your fervour can cope with. Alternatively, some Westerners have done this and remain committed to this day.

When done wisely, ordination can be a pathway that supports your meditation practice to develop to higher places.

CHAPTER TEN

Donations

When searching around for a retreat to sign up for, you'll notice some cost money and some are donation-only. Of the ones that charge money up front, some are profit-based while others are charging only enough to cover their costs.

The donation-only centres really do depend on our generosity to maintain their facilities and pay their bills. So, while no one is likely to ever prompt you to pay, it's obviously important we recognise our tacit role in this relationship and give back in accordance with what we receive.

The word *dāna* comes from the ancient Indian languages of Pali and Sanskrit, meaning gift or to deal out, and these days it is used interchangeably with donation or service. It's interesting that this Pali term probably has links to European languages thanks to the Proto-Indo-European root *dō*, to give, via the Latin word *dōno*, meaning to give gifts or to bestow, which in turn has influenced European languages through verbs such as *donate* in English, *donner* in French, *donar* in Spanish, and so on. Clearly it has been an important and commonly shared concept across regions, cultures, and millennia.

In traditional Asian Buddhist cultural settings, to give *dāna* to the monastery or to a monk or nun is to accrue good *kamma* (Sanskrit: *karma*) as well as merit for yourself and your family. So it's an activity people go out of their way to practise enthusiastically rather than something they feel obliged to do out of custom. In Sri Lanka, for example, community groups hire buses to go on a day trip to their favourite monastery where they cook and serve up the day's two meals for the monks and nuns. At such occasions there is joy all around as the laypeople serve, assist, give to the monastics, and bring forward even their smallest children to join in the joyful spiritual act of giving and supporting others.

If you're coming to a meditation practice environment from outside such a cultural background, please do keep in mind that these centres depend on people and community groups to keep them going through giving supplies, cash, and services such as repair work. In short, if you stay at the centre, you really should leave a donation when you depart, despite the fact no one explicitly requests it. Having said all of that, a handful of meditation centres require an "advance donation" of a fixed amount per night's stay, probably out of concern that international visitors are not aware of *dāna* customs.

Some people new to *dāna* ask me about figures. *How much is right to give?* It's a well-meant question because nobody wants to give too little. But there's no hard and fast rule. Over the years I sometimes gave lavishly when I felt well-off enough to do so, and at other times I went away feeling stingy that I might have short-changed the centre. So I eventually found a way to answer the question for myself: I give as much as allows me to sleep well. As simple as that. If you do a rough calculation of what it costs in the local economy for the centre to host you (food, electricity, wear and tear) and then double it, I think you're on the right track.

You may have noticed that no payment for the teachers has so far been mentioned. In traditional settings, teachers are typically monks or nuns who don't receive payment for their efforts. Supporting the monastery or meditation centre is enough. In a Western setting, you may be notified during the application procedure that a donation for the teacher's time is appreciated. These teachers are usually laypeople who give up their professional or personal time to teach you, so any gift you wish to leave them helps to offset the cost of their teaching time taking them away from paid work.

Note all of the above relates to developing country circumstances. Meditation centres in Western countries usually have much higher overhead costs and so may charge a fixed daily fee, or have a minimum donation requirement, or a lump sum fee to be paid upon booking. And these rates tend to be many times higher than in Asian countries. If you are used to paying such amounts, you will find it no trouble to be generous at monasteries in Asia.

CHAPTER ELEVEN

Visas and international travel

Let's talk travel. First, most countries require you to have a visa in order to spend time there. Second, a standard tourist visa or visa on arrival may not be long enough for your intended stay. And third, there may be some logistical challenges in getting to and from the places you want to train in.

Visas can be divided into three main types. Note that your nationality will determine the specifics as these conditions are not universally applicable to all passports.

1. On entry or on arrival. This is a visa that the immigration officer in the airport or port of entry stamps or inserts into your passport. It is typically free. This is the simplest and least troublesome type of visa. Examples: Hong Kong, Thailand, Singapore, Malaysia.
2. Apply on entry/online. This type of visa usually involves filling out a form at the immigration area and paying a fee. There may be a choice of visa types and lengths at differing prices, so it's worth investigating before departure. Increasingly it is possible to apply online before departure. You usually need a passport photo or two and may require cash in either United States dollars or the local

currency. Airport visa counters now often accept credit cards and a range of currencies. Examples: Sri Lanka, Nepal.
3. Apply in advance. This is the most inconvenient and old-fashioned type of visa. You are required to send your passport and application form to a consular office in your home country or to go visit an office in person. It can take time, involve a variety of paperwork, and possibly also involve added costs such as courier fees. Note that such countries are mostly transitioning to make these visas available through an online application process, and so may end up in type 2 above. Examples: China, India, Myanmar.

Here's where some travel experience can make a difference. It just so happens that, when you apply for a visa through the consular office in your home country, you may face a longer, more onerous, and more costly process than if you apply in another country on your way to the destination, or if you apply in the airport on arrival. Be sure to look up the immigration department website of the country you want to visit, as well as well-regarded travel information websites, rather than visit the website of the consular office in your home country.

Let's look at an example, but please note visa regulations change regularly and differ depending on the passport you are carrying. If I intend to travel to China, and I apply while I'm still in Australia, I may be required to submit a complete set of documents regarding my return flights, my accommodation bookings, and my funds available for the visit. I may even be required to show a police report proving I have no criminal history. Then there is a fee, not to mention courier costs. Alternatively, if I stop over in Hong Kong for a couple of days of sightseeing on the way to mainland China, I can quickly get a visa through any travel agent in the city with no supporting documents and for a lower fee. (Of course, staying in Hong Kong has its own costs.)

While you can enter countries to do meditation training on a regular tourist visa, one country is a stark exception: Myanmar. This country, once known (and still known to Americans) as Burma, has been the home of high quality meditation training for many decades, but it has also been notoriously closed, cut off, or under some form of unrest or oppression for much of that time. Throughout these difficult times, the government's attitude to foreigners has been one of wary, begrudging tolerance.

If you are not turned off yet and still want to travel there for training, you are required to get a "religious" visa in advance for meditation purposes. The good news is it's quick and easy and inexpensive if you factor in a short stay in Bangkok on the way. Considering your flight in and out of Myanmar is likely to go through Bangkok, it's not an inconvenience to stop over. You only need to fill out a form, attach a passport photo, and pay a fee. Then you return the next day to pick it up. The visa grants a seventy-day stay and can be extended by the meditation centre while you remain in training. So while it's a small hindrance at the start, you are then well set up to stay and train as much as you like.

Other Asian countries have length limitations. For example, you can get a free thirty-day stamp in your passport on arrival in Thailand, but if you want to meditate longer than that, you need to obtain a longer visa prior to entering the country. On the other hand, Sri Lanka now offers a six-month visa online prior to arrival, allowing you lots of time for training.

Generally, visas are an old holdover from earlier times when we needed paper documents to traverse national boundaries. I believe they're quickly becoming a thing of the past so you may find less and less inconvenience as the years go by. Whatever the case, don't let a simple bureaucratic measure hold you back from going to those countries to seek out high quality training opportunities. As with other aspects of the meditation journey, the greatest benefits often lie on the other side of a challenge.

CHAPTER TWELVE

A day on retreat

To finish up this section, let's take a look at how a hypothetical day on retreat might unfold ...

You awake to the sound of a bell. It's dark and silent. You're feeling cosy in your single bed and don't want to get up. A glance at the clock: 4am! You're tempted to roll over and go back to sleep. But remembering why you're here, you get up and begin your morning routine.

Outside it's still dark. You notice other meditators emerging from nearby doors and shuffling towards the Meditation Hall in the cold night air. In the hall, it's a hushed atmosphere, people are quietly moving themselves into position on their cushions and some are bowing solemnly to the front of the hall. Occasionally there's a sneeze or a cough, but overall it's a quiet and reverential scene. Despite how early it is and how sleepy you're feeling, you are pleased to have made the commitment to be here.

From the outset you find this first session challenging. The mind continually recalls how comfortable and warm the bed was and goes off into daydreams. You bring your attention back to the object of meditation, zooming in on the sensations of the breath and striving to stay there. It's not long before you find the mind lost in some memory from long ago and you gently call it back to the breath. Only seconds later you notice the mind finding a thought more interesting than the breath and starting to go off wandering again. There is a moment of satisfaction that your mindfulness is alert enough to have seen that happening.

After some time has passed, a bell rings to signal breakfast. Immediately there is shuffling in the hall and soon you're all moving in silent single file across the grounds in the pre-dawn glow to one of your favourite places in the whole centre: the Dining Hall!

Inside, everyone moves quietly and slowly, trying to pay attention to each moment while also trying not to get in each other's way. You fill your plate with food from the buffet, grab a mug of your favourite drink, and go find a place at one of the tables. There is a constant buzz of background noises—clinking of cutlery and shunting of chairs—but otherwise the mood is subdued. The absence of voices in such a crowded room is striking.

Afterwards, you walk back to the accommodation where you sweep the room interior as well as the path out front. Then the bell rings again to signal the start of the morning session.

Back in the hall the mood is a little different. People are more focused and energetic now. You bring attention again to your meditation object and work intently on staying there. As the morning progresses, you notice changes in the way the mind perceives the object and the way it reacts to such events as disturbances in the hall. All of these observations seem new, an advance from what you were experiencing yesterday. You reflect on how interesting this is and how much you're learning, and inevitably the mind drifts to conversations you'd like to have after the retreat, telling everyone about your time here. You become engrossed in these conversations until, like suddenly awaking from a dream, you catch the mind busily thinking and immediately bring the attention back to the object, reflecting for a moment on how much you seem to enjoy daydreaming.

Just as the ache in your legs is getting so strong that you're thinking about standing up for a break, the bell rings and this time everyone moves off to the Dining Hall for lunch. The hall is a bit noisier this time as everyone's hunger is stronger after the morning's training and the wonderful smells filling the room prompt everyone to move with a little more haste. While eating, you notice how strongly the mind is observing every detail with interest, the taste of each mouthful, the texture of the food, the sensations of swallowing it, and also the movements and behaviour of the other people in the room.

After lunch you take a walk through the grounds, arrive back at your room, and wash some clothes in a big plastic basin in the attached bathroom. When done, you hang them outside on the clothes line, noticing the post-lunch sluggishness beginning to drag you down. You make some notes in your journal about how the meditation practice has gone so far today and then catch yourself daydreaming again. You resist the temptation to lie down. The experience of past days has taught you that sleepiness sets in quickly when lying prone and then going back to the meditation is even harder.

It's an hour since you finished lunch and the bell signals the start of the afternoon session. In the Meditation Hall you notice a few people are absent. Maybe they're lying down or maybe they're advanced students allowed to practise in their own rooms. Again, some people are nodding off from the drowsiness so common after a big meal. Your afternoon session starts off a little drowsy too, but you know from recent experience what to do: continually bringing your attention back to the object over and over, eventually overcoming the sleepiness. As the afternoon progresses you notice again how your perception of the object of your meditation has evolved and is now revealing a different aspect of the experience. You take some encouragement from this and push on, time and again overcoming the natural inclination of the mind to wander to past events, future plans, and daydreaming about what might have been. There are some periods when the mind seems to quieten, to zoom in and stay there, and occasionally you even notice the body and external distractions have mostly vanished. These moments seem imbued with peace and calm, even a subtle joy.

Being Thursday, at 3pm you leave the hall and walk mindfully across the grounds to the Interview Room, where you have a twice-weekly meeting with the teacher. You wait your turn outside the door and enter when called, bowing three times to the floor in front of the teacher. This is your only time to use your vocal cords each week so the interview often starts off with a little bit of awkward throat-clearing and small talk.

You describe what you've been doing in the practice and explain some of the changes you've noticed. The teacher is encouraging, saying you're showing clear signs of progress and are moving along in the development of the practice. Then the teacher points out you've been getting a little tied up in this or that distraction and should remind yourself, when these things happen, to let them go and return to the main aim of the practice. You realise this is a good point, something you'd missed, and you thank the teacher while looking forward to polishing up your technique. The teacher bids you farewell with some encouraging words and you leave after another three bows, holding open the door for the next meditator.

In the hall, for the last part of the daytime schedule, you bring a renewed determination and enthusiasm to the practice and notice what you think may be some points of development as the afternoon progresses. But you also recall the teacher warning you off speculating on how your practice is progressing, so you quickly drop these thoughts and come back to the breath. There is a lot of tiredness and pain in the legs now, after many hours of sitting without moving. Around sunset there is a break for juice in the Dining Hall and as you sip the cup of sugar and lime, noticing cascades of intense sensations in the body and reactions in the mind, you reflect on how even such simple activities yield layers and levels of intrigue for a mind in training. You reflect how, if you were outside the retreat, you'd notice none of these intricate experiences and how they make you feel more alive than ever before, and you again feel gratitude for having given this a try. Shortly after, it's back to the Meditation Hall in the dusk light for the evening's proceedings.

When everyone has settled on their cushions, silence descends on the room. The teacher enters and takes his or her seat on the podium at the front. The teacher gives a preliminary explanation and begins chanting. Everyone chants together, some reading from a booklet, others from memory.

For the next hour the teacher delivers a lecture on a topic of relevance to the meditation practice and occasionally links it up with matters of life outside the retreat. Specifically, tonight the teacher addresses the issue of energy and effort, and how to be on your guard about the onset of lethargy and sleepiness. The teacher mentions snoring in the hall to humorous effect and makes a few jokes that poke fun at the misunderstandings you all tend to bring to the practice. It feels good to laugh together in this otherwise austere and silent environment. The solitude of the retreat can be challenging at times, so it's comforting to share with the others some light-hearted moments.

After the talk, the meditators bow three times to the teacher who then departs.

The final sitting session of the evening is challenging as the mind inclines to thoughts of that warm and comfortable bed not so far away. Several times your chin touches your chest and your head jerks back up as you snap back to consciousness. You sit up straight and breathe deeply to energise yourself. You've learnt from the teacher these sessions are more productive than they seem because the mind's meandering activities are somewhat weakened and so absorption into the object of meditation can occur more effortlessly. You persevere and don't leave until the clock has finally reached 9pm and everyone begins drifting outside.

Back at the room, you bring in the washing, make a few more notes in your journal, catch yourself daydreaming again, and take a shower. It's now 10pm, and after lying down in the dark, you notice the mind is more energetic than you thought while in the hall and the meditation practice seems to be humming along on its own as you lie there. It's surprising and pleasing to find your practice has gained so much momentum that the mind is absorbed in it no matter what you're doing. Finally, you drift off to sleep.

INTERLUDE 1

Concentration meditation instructions

This is the most basic exercise. But basic is not the same as easy. The original name in the Pali language is *Ānāpānasati*, literally meaning "inhale-exhale mindfulness". The objective is to maintain consistent attention on the sensations of the breath as it comes in and as it goes out. Traditionally this method is practised around the nostrils or upper lip, so let's stick to those two areas.

When you have sat comfortably in your chosen posture in a quiet place, relax the body and allow the breath to settle into its routine.

Remember:

> *At no time should we manipulate or force the breath in any way.*
> *We are here to observe things happening, not to make things happen.*

Now bring your attention to the front of your face and narrow it down to the area of the nose and its immediate surroundings. Think of the area encompassed by a sphere an inch in diameter centring on the tip of your nose. Look for the clearest appearance of sensations of the breath coming in and going out on the rims of the nostrils or in the space between the upper lip and the nostrils. It may take a few cycles of the breath to find something. Patience is key at all stages in all forms of meditation. So just take your time and enjoy the chance to sit quietly and peacefully without the need to do anything. Once you begin to notice sensations there, gently hold your attention there and stay present with it from the beginning of the breath to the end.

At any time, when you discover the attention has wandered and is thinking or looking at some other aspect of your experience, let go and bring the attention back. Our minds think, just like our lungs breathe. We shouldn't be surprised or disappointed to find this. So just let go of the thought, bring the attention back, and push on. This cycle of discovering the attention has wandered then bringing it back will occur countless times. The key is to notice it and bring it back, not to try to fight it. Let's view the straying attention like an inquisitive puppy or kitten that wanders around exploring. Without any anger or agitation, we gently pick it up and put it back where it belongs, over and over.

When your attention is squarely on the sensations of the breath, try to maintain it there from one moment to the next, over and over, without a break. Rather than noticing there is a breath coming in and then going off to think about something, let's instead keep the attention there, remaining aware throughout each movement: from the start of the movement of a breath, through its middle moments, all the way to the conclusion of that movement. There may be a few moments of nothing between breaths so let's just maintain the attention there and then follow the sensations again as the breath goes through the next full movement.

That's it. Just keep that up until the bell rings. Let me reiterate this is not easy, and in the early stages you will find that your attention wanders far more than it stays put. This is completely natural and is not at all an indication that you are no good at meditation. There has never been a human in the world who hasn't struggled with maintaining attention during meditation. With time, you will get better at it and see changes occur in the experience of the breath, the mind, and the body.

Summary. Observe the breath at the edges of the nostrils or above the upper lip. Keep the attention on the sensations there all the way from the beginning to the end of each breath movement. When the attention wanders, gently bring it back.

Advanced tip. If you find you can zoom in and watch the breath for many seconds at a time, bring attention to finer and finer details such as the precise moment the breath begins and ends, as well as watch a smaller and smaller area of sensation. Precision and consistency are the two parameters we want to develop here. Beware of getting attached to or engrossed in anything that occurs in the practice. This will not help with your progress.

PART II

RETREATS: MENTAL

All of humanity's problems stem from man's inability to sit quietly in a room alone.

—Blaise Pascal, philosopher

CHAPTER THIRTEEN

Preparing yourself

It's not true that you need a well-established meditation practice before your first retreat, but it is true that you should do a short retreat for your first attempt. In my opinion, a short retreat is ten to fourteen days and a long retreat is a month or more.

This is based on the reasoning that not all days on retreat are equal. Most people need several days to settle into the retreat routine and it's also possible the last day is spent tidying up and making arrangements to leave. So ten days is a good minimum to aim for to gain benefits. At the upper end, there is no limit: some monastics have been known to spend years in retreat.

Please don't misunderstand the point here. Of course, any amount of meditation practice is better than none. If a three-day retreat is available to you, by all means, dive in! Even this short stint helps you develop skills and inspiration for later retreats. It all adds up.

Once we're at the retreat, some unique conditions might confront us: silence, solitude, intense mental focus, withdrawal from all our normal life distractions and enjoyments. In such an atmosphere, we may find that whatever themes were bubbling under the surface of our normal daily life, they jump out and surprise us with great vividness and energy. As such, any lingering regrets, disputes, or unfinished business can become a big deal once we are cut off from the outside world.

We should take care of all preparatory matters before the retreat. Most obvious is to lock in all the travel and logistical arrangements in advance. Seeking permission to use the internet halfway through the retreat because you need to book a hotel or an onward flight is not going to help your training. Another tip is to say farewell to everyone, especially folks who need to know you won't be in touch during the coming silent weeks or months.

If you've had some kind of difficulties with your partner or relative or workmate, consider taking time out to settle these matters before the retreat begins. To be stranded in a retreat with a conversation going round and round in your head that should've been had before you went offline, or that you are determined to have when you get back, can be disturbing and destructive of your practice. You'll find, as stated later in the section on the Five Hindrances, regrets and worries are powerful obstructions to meditation practice.

Please do not take these matters lightly as you'll have plenty of time on retreat to be bothered by them and regret not having done something beforehand. You'll be doing yourself a very big favour.

Consider the following disruptive scenarios.

- Once on retreat you discover an important anniversary or birthday is coming up and you didn't leave a message or gift to commemorate it. Now you feel a need to reach out to that person.
- You hadn't begun making bookings for your family's Christmas travels, and it might be too late by the time you leave the retreat. Now you want to leave the retreat to get online.
- You didn't leave adequate instructions with the colleague who will handle your work responsibilities while you're away. Now you're thinking about all the things that could go wrong at work.
- You committed to a future social event, but forgot to cancel once you booked the retreat. You desperately want to contact that person.

The same goes for normal life concerns such as paying bills or leaving funds with others to settle bills for us. Consider how it would feel to be on a one-month retreat and halfway through you realise you hadn't paid the rent. In the pin-drop silent setting of a retreat, such minor matters can explode into a major drama. So make a to-do list and clear them up prior to starting out.

After experiences like these, it'll become clear why, for many people, the monastic life offers an effective setting for advancing in meditation training. Most of those areas of life that can curse us laypeople with regrets and worries during training would be largely left at the gate if we shaved our heads and donned the robes for good. Of course, being a monk or nun is more complicated than that, but there are good reasons why some people choose to go all the way. To get some experience yourself, temporary ordination is common at meditation centres in Myanmar and Thailand. See the chapter on ordination on retreat.

And finally, once all of the matters you can control are dealt with, it's a good idea to settle into an attitude of letting go of everything else for the time you'll be away. All those other life matters will still be there when you return, and you won't suffer for being free from them for a while. Just don't forget the email auto-reply and voicemail message.

CHAPTER FOURTEEN

Commitment vs. Quitting

One prominent meditation organisation gives you multiple reminders during the online application process that you are committing to stay and complete the entire retreat. Upon arrival and check-in, they remind you again. And on the first evening before the training begins, they state that anyone who is having doubts is welcome to leave. After all those warnings, it is assumed you're good to go. But, despite all of these steps, it is common for some people to leave before the ten-day retreat is over.

Why? Is it really that hard to see a retreat through?

While a meditation retreat can be hard work and usually requires a lot of striving to overcome obstacles and hindrances, it really isn't *that* hard. The great majority of people do see it through. So while you need to bring some degree of dedication and determination to the task, you needn't fear that it is beyond the capabilities of normal people like you and me.

In my opinion the most common cause of early departure is simply not being prepared to give it a firm go. Some people go to retreats like a runner who turns up to a marathon undecided about whether they really want to finish or just go home early. As you'll surely discover, anything but a clear determination to stick it out will become unhelpful during the long hours of silent practice.

A reliable defence against this kind of wavering and possible surrender is to establish in your mind a rock-solid commitment to the entire time frame: whether it's as short as a week, or as long as a month or more. No ifs or buts. No wiggle room. Zero tolerance of doubting. No backing down. That kind of thing. This is why it's a good idea that your first retreat be fairly short: it's easier to commit to with confidence.

A key point of practice wisdom is:

> *The attitude we bring to the practice is as important as the practice itself.*

To approach the retreat in the right frame of mind is guaranteed to set you up for better results. Resolving to see it through, setting aside the necessary time to be free from daily life concerns, and keeping in mind the benefits of completing a meditation retreat: all of this should contribute to the determination and enthusiasm needed to overcome the challenges you'll face from time to time.

What challenges?

There will be experiences unlike anything you've known before, both positive and difficult, so it's possible to be caught out, to be surprised, and to turn to thoughts of quitting. I'm not just referring to the rare but possible peak experiences such as mystical insights, extreme bliss, or explosions of sensations, or at the other end of the scale the potential for fearful or anxious moments. Instead, sometimes it could just be hours of amazement at how much patience is required to sit still, deal with the incredible depths of boredom that can assail you, and not get up and leave. There's also the surprising intensity of craving for distraction, for anything but sitting still another moment. And don't forget there is the inevitable discovery of the astounding amount of aimless and unhelpful thinking that the mind is capable of.

This and more will confront you from day one. So developing the mental commitment to sit with it, sit through it, weather it, and eventually overcome it (or overcome the aversion to it) is the best protection you can have.

It also helps to consider that your comfort zone—that place you inhabit in daily life surrounded by familiar people, items, routines, and habits—will be far away and out of reach. You may discover dimensions to losing your comfort zone you never knew before. Like the awkwardness of chanting in a foreign language, bowing to a teacher or statue, sitting in an unusual posture, walking so slowly you almost fall over from disorientation, eating strange food, getting by on little sleep, and so on. Picture yourself not being able to keep up your comforting daily routines: like that gourmet coffee you enjoy every morning; or your favourite social media scrolling; or endless hot showers. Add to all that the new and unusual sensory and psychological experiences that come from hours on the cushion. So, before setting out, remind yourself there may be things that will come up which require a greater degree of calm, patience, and determination than you're used to applying to regular activities.

Another hard-won lesson of my years on retreat, and from which I gain boundless encouragement, is this basic principle: *whatever happens on retreat is just practice-related*. This apparently mundane statement means, whether it's bodily discomfort, disturbed sleep, strange or unpleasant mental states, constipation, impatience, doubt about the teacher or the method, excessive sexual ruminating, agitation towards the other meditators, boredom, confounded over-thinking of long-ago events, that growing desire to quit your job or relationship and go become a holy one by the Ganges, and much more, it's all arising because of the training you're currently going through. It's not because of something you did or failed to do, or because you've lived an unhappy life, or your body can't take the training, or any other self-directed blame. It's because intensive meditation training reaches deep inside us and flips switches and pulls strings that give rise to new or awkward experiences. So, back to the same old refrain: bring a strong degree of calm, patient determination, and you'll sail through it all just fine.

At any stage, if you find you're watching the minute hand on the clock and wondering how to see through the remaining hours and days, here's another basic principle discovered through years of training: *the time passes fastest when you knuckle down and do the meditation*. An afternoon can drag by painfully or fly by comfortably depending on where you direct your energy and attention.

After some experience, I developed a helpful method for the longer, more arduous retreats. I took a pad of multicoloured sticky notes and wrote all manner of inspirational reminders, quotes from the Buddhist texts, as well as quotes from my teachers during the retreat, and stuck them all over a door or wall panel in my room. Of course, they were not for decoration or distraction, but to look at when needed. So whenever

I felt the training was weighing heavily and my stamina was running low, I would step up to the wall for a few moments of inspirational self-encouragement.

The final advice is that if you are struggling and feeling unable to go on—this can happen for a number of reasons so don't beat yourself up—then take a break and go for a walk in the grounds or a lie-down on your bed. And if that doesn't help, find the teacher and have a chat. He or she may give you some helpful advice or agree that it's time for you to finish up.

Whichever way it goes for you, please don't berate yourself for not making it. There are times when we just aren't ready to give what a retreat demands of us, and there is no shame in finally accepting this. You can always return and try again some other day.

CHAPTER FIFTEEN

Devices

An area of contention about retreats that I think will only worsen with the years is that of digital device usage. It can be a matter of individual addiction, but it is also generational. For those of us who remember life before devices, we have a baseline to refer to when facing up to letting go of them and spending some weeks or months without them. But for younger folks who've only ever known life with a device in hand, giving it up for any period at all might seem unbearably difficult. The unfortunate result is that many people work up a justification to keep their device handy throughout the retreat.

Let me be clear on this:

> *If you use a mobile device during your retreat training,*
> *it* will *undermine your practice.*

Since you've come all this way and set aside all other parts of your life for the purpose of this retreat, a serious and respectful approach to the training would include getting rid of the device.

If we practise Noble Silence to support our training but then spend periods each day responding to emails, chatting with friends and family, scrolling through social media feeds, and scouring news websites, rest assured it will fill our minds with complicated ponderings, daydreams, and adverse reactions. Our devices and their apps are cleverly designed to be addictive. That need to check and see what's been going on since you last looked at it minutes ago is a learned response that funds big tech firms and their advertisers. That Fear Of Missing Out on what everyone else out there off-retreat is doing is no accident: instilling FOMO in you is the design goal of social media systems as well as the devices we view them on. That craving for taking the mind away from the present moment is also no accident: it's a human instinct, and meditation training is intended to overcome it. So playing around with your device means undoing everything you're there to achieve.

I've been to meditation centres across the range of policies. There are places that require you to hand in a phone during check-in. There are places that recommend you hand it in and provide a secure way to store it, but it's up to you. And there are places that don't mention it and leave it to you to manage this aspect of your retreat.

So I've tried the different options. There's locking it away in the office for the duration of the retreat. There's keeping the phone and SIM card separate to make it more trouble to use it and thereby reduce the likelihood. There's putting the phone away in a bag and hoping to forget about it. And there's leaving it out in full view where the temptation is ever-present.

The conclusion was clear: anything but locking it away in the office was a distraction that undermined my training. When keeping it in my room, merely knowing the device could be accessed if a suitable rationale could be dreamt up meant the mind turned to seeking just such a justification. For example, I would think a lot about post-retreat travel arrangements and then get online to make bookings. But if I took the other path and locked the phone away for safe-keeping with no way to get it back (except in an emergency), this had a liberating effect. I simply never stopped to think about it for the whole retreat. Out of reach, out of mind.

A few years back I served among the volunteers at a popular meditation centre in Australia and we all noticed an interesting trend. The half-dozen people who ended up finding the retreat too demanding and quit early were also the ones who'd refused to check their devices in for safe-keeping and had been using them throughout the training. Probably not a coincidence!

I expect my rant on this topic won't change everyone's minds because for some of us the addiction runs deep. But why not try this: on your next retreat, experiment by going completely without the device and see what happens. You may find the same as me: once it's locked away, you never spare a thought for it again and you may even begin to delight in the freedom its absence gives you. I usually get to the last day of a retreat and discover I'm fearful of getting the phone back. All those emails and messages demanding an immediate response will rattle my hard-earned peace of mind in no time. In the end, these are valuable lessons to take back to our daily life.

CHAPTER SIXTEEN

East and West

Apologies for the use of these outdated terms, but it is a common view that Buddhism is inherently Asian (or "Eastern") and therefore people coming to meditation from "Western" countries are engaging in cross-cultural practices. Sure, there are cultural differences, but they aren't the biggest challenge. The mind consists of deeper levels than culture and language, and it is at those levels that meditation does its work.

If it's true you are from outside a traditional Asian cultural background, it's likely you'll be leaving your cultural comfort zone to attend a retreat at a centre either in an Asian country or that has been influenced by such traditional approaches to meditation training. As mentioned elsewhere in the book, being ready to leave your normal cultural, social, and lifestyle routines behind is an important preparation for your retreat.

The first big difference you'll likely notice is that Asian Buddhists approach the teachings and the practice with deep reverence, including traditional religious sentiments such as faith and devotion. On the other hand, Western meditators may attend a retreat to kick the tyres of the method or to find some kind of preconceived self-centred goal. We could think of these differing approaches as representing a religious versus materialistic divide. The former is driven by a view that the practice helps improve one's spiritual conditions in this world and also in future lives, as well as contributing to an overall raising of humanity. It is a long time frame with few short-term goals. The latter perspective is usually seeking a specific, somewhat quantifiable outcome such as psychological or spiritual development along a particular axis. It is usually short-term in outlook and seeks something like changes in one's degree of satisfaction with life. While they are both based on assumptions and are assisted and hindered by the preconceptions they each bring to the practice, it's fair to say the former approach tends to lead to more progress because there are fewer misgivings and hesitations on the part of the religiously devoted.

Another expression of cultural differences that you may encounter is segregation by sex. In some major meditation traditions, males and females are strictly separated, although they may share a meditation hall. Generally, the more modern and secular the centre, the less such segregation is practised. And in some centres, men and women eat and meditate in the same spaces and might even stay in the same buildings, albeit still separated to some extent. So the approach differs depending on the underlying cultural assumptions.

This kind of segregation may seem behind the times to some of us now, but in some cultures, to encourage women to attend meditation training, a centre would have to establish a completely separate area for women so that families had confidence that their female relatives were going to be safe. I think we can agree that's all very noble and worthwhile in those specific contexts.

On a different topic, when some meditators travel to a foreign country for a retreat, they may find themselves on a wildly spiritual quest that wreaks havoc with their worldviews and they may lose all sense of what's appropriate. They might remove items of clothing and wander around, or go barefoot for the entire retreat, or pull exotic yoga poses in public areas, or go AWOL outside the centre to explore the nearby streets and communities. The list goes on. I've also witnessed or heard of foreign meditators overcome with energetic spells who race around under the blazing sun wearing only their lower garments. Or who lie down outdoors for no apparent reason, chattering to themselves. Or lock themselves in their room all day, or suddenly decide to go on a fast, or shave off their eyebrows. Or argue with the teacher for not seeing how awakened they've become. Or go around advising strangers on what they think is wrong with their practice. Or decide they've suddenly seen through everything, don't need to practice anymore, and grab their things and leave. Or, as incredible as it sounds, I witnessed a guy gradually remove his clothing piece by piece during an evening sitting session until he was completely naked, laid out on the floor. Fortunately, it was a men-only monastery, and the lights in the hall were low so most people didn't notice. Please note that apart from all of these behaviours being weird in any context, they can be viewed as extremely inappropriate by the traditional Buddhists who host us. There is one major meditation centre in Myanmar where foreign meditators are sectioned off in a separate area. The teacher only occasionally bothers to go there for interviews because we are not taken seriously as meditators. And while this is very unfortunate and undesirable, after seeing what goes on sometimes, it may not be undeserved.

A meditation retreat in a foreign country is not a holiday camp, nor is it all about offloading our latent psychological difficulties on the people around us or "finding ourselves" in ways that are detrimental to the needs of the rest of the community for a quiet and respectful meditation space. In a traditional Buddhist setting, a meditation retreat is a solemn religious or soteriological undertaking. We are there to participate in the freeing of ourselves from ignorance, and institutionally we are granted the chance to train with a view to raising the spiritual quality of the human species. The bottom line: please let's all respect the local culture and save going off the rails for outside the retreat.

Other differences an outsider may notice, depending on the tradition and cultural setting, are reverential practices towards the Buddha, his teachings, and the monastics who represent his legacy. In most Asian cultures, for instance, it's customary to bow to the Buddha statue by touching our head on the floor whenever entering a room. Outside such a context, this "kowtowing" gesture may look demeaning, but it is simply considered the appropriate way to show respect to a very high ideal. Buddhists view the Buddha as the most important person to have lived in our historical epoch, and his teachings represent for them the only light in a darkened world. So showing a high degree of respect each time one comes before his likeness is considered an important practice.

To bow, meditators kneel on the floor and place their forehead and hands three times on the floor in front of them. They may also do this again when departing the room. You'll notice as a retreat progresses, most meditators take up the practice. If you're unsure about joining in, that's fine. No one demands it of anyone. But you could consider that traditional meditation training involves weakening the hold of unwholesome mental habits on our minds. And practising letting go of conceit so as to revere the memory of a highly respected teacher is one way of travelling this path. Give it a try and see where it leads for you.

In a traditional setting, teachers are usually monks and nuns, and are highly revered. When a person has given up lay life and entered the monastic community, it is a given that he or she is respected as a representative of the Buddha's way. I admit to a little personal discomfort at having to demonstrate deep reverence for someone I don't know and have only just met, but it's another example of letting go of our cultural assumptions in order to fully experience the retreat. The robed person in question is not necessarily the reason for bowing. It is the teacher's status as a representative of an epoch-making tradition that we pay respect to. When looked at appropriately, bowing becomes easy.

The expected behaviour towards a teacher usually involves bowing with the forehead to the floor both at the start and end of any conversation. It may also involve holding the hands together in a prayer gesture in front of the chest throughout any dealings with the teacher. These practices tend to be customary among traditional Buddhists, but the good news is that a newcomer is usually forgiven for not keeping up with them. If in doubt, ask around about what is customary, or just watch what others do.

While contrasting traditional and Western perspectives, I'd like to touch on a topic that some Western meditators have raised with me. They report taking up the practice of intensive meditation only to find their friends and family do not understand their motivations and are not supportive.

To go abroad to participate in a meditation retreat, especially a long one, requires the realignment of life priorities. Our studies, careers, financial goals, or other responsibilities have to be put on hold for a time, and this can raise eyebrows among those who don't see the value in what we're working on. There might be questions or conversations that are uncomfortable. There may even be resistance and pushing back against our plans. And this is not always straightforward to deal with, as our reasons and motivations may not be completely clear even to ourselves. We may simply be following an ineffable subconscious drive, a sense that things are not quite right with our existence and that a deeper, wider-ranging search is required. So those conversations could be challenging.

First of all, there's no blanket solution. Individual relationships, cultural backgrounds, and life stages are all important considerations and differ from person to person. It is worth noting the earliest Buddhist texts tell of many examples of people who set out to follow the Buddha's way by abandoning the "householder life" to become a monk or nun under his guidance. Those ancient individuals also ran into significant difficulties with their families. The old stories usually describe an emotional struggle culminating in a hunger strike or similarly extreme rebellion, after which the parents tearfully agree to let their son or daughter leave their house—and effectively leave the family and community—for an entirely new life. So it is not the case that the resistance or lack of support from those closest to us is only a modern Western phenomenon. We could say the fault line here is more between the spiritual and non-spiritual viewpoints.

In my opinion, there are only two steps for tackling this state of affairs. The first is to appeal to those close to us through open and respectful communication. We should explain it the best we can, recommend a book or podcast to clarify it, or encourage them to try meditation for themselves. You could also take some time to summarise for yourself why intensive meditation training is so important, then find ways to explain that to others. I have heard of meditators referring to their family's religious heritage, such as by drawing comparisons and suggesting the principles of Buddhism are not at odds with their own religion.

Second, if after these attempts the people in our lives are still not able to appreciate the motivation behind our efforts, then it is time to accept we are on our own. Of course, you could back down to appease them. But if you are deeply driven, this will ultimately not work out and you will find yourself returning to investigate meditation another time, maybe with an added sense of resentment. In the meantime, to pursue fulfilment in life, it is sometimes necessary to listen only to our best instincts even if the result is to walk alone.

On the bright side, as we go deeper into our new interest, we are likely to encounter more and more people who share our desire, and such friendships will be important in finding our feet on the new path. The Buddha and his closest followers were reported to have spoken much of the value of "spiritual friendship". So I would encourage you to seek out companionship and moral support among other like-minded people. It is possible to find groups to sit with and there are also online means for connecting up with meditators.

Despite what seem like vast cultural differences, in fact the Buddha's teachings and the related meditation methods are a universal human heritage and require no identifying into (or appropriating) other cultures or religions. By paying attention, deeper truths are revealed to us. That's it. It's unhelpful and stigmatising to view it as East versus West. The best we can hope for is that the people around us find our enthusiasm infectious, or at least appreciate the importance of these investigations to us and, out of that, develop respect for what we are working on.

* * *

A friend once asked me to suggest a book to help her in her meditation practice. Considering her meditation interests, I recommended a title by Ajahn Brahm, the British-born, Thai-trained monk now resident in Australia. She frowned. "Can't you recommend an Asian teacher?" Later, I sent her a copy of the book, but I doubt she read it.

The idea that Buddhist meditation is inherently "Eastern" or Asian is as vague as it is unhelpful. No one who is considered Buddhist today is proven to share any ethnic or cultural background with the Buddha himself, who came from the Sakyan people of the Himalayan foothills, who were vanquished in warfare long ago and, as far as we know, the survivors absorbed into neighbouring kingdoms. Modern Buddhists neither speak the language he spoke nor walk through the same world he once did. I would even suggest that, for example, Buddhism travelling from ancient India to pre-medieval Japan is a greater cultural leap than from Japan to North America and Europe in our times.

This is not to diminish the immense sacrifice and efforts of countless people over many centuries who devoted their lives to the study, translation, and teaching of the knowledge and practices to ensure their survival. We modern learners absolutely owe a colossal debt of gratitude. But a more helpful way to look upon the development of Buddhism is that the teachings have spread across diverse regions and cultures, and the current engagement with new regions and cultures in our times is just a natural continuation of this spread. The fact the teachings have travelled so far from their origins is testament to how universally applicable they are.

The moral of the story is that great ideas are highly infectious and are bound to travel far and wide. So while getting to grips with the Buddhist teachings involves learning words and concepts from past and foreign cultures, they ultimately point to something deeper than language and culture. Anyone, regardless of their origins, who invests sufficient effort can come to a mastery of them.

CHAPTER SEVENTEEN

Teachers

Every retreat has at least one teacher and they may become the centre of your retreat experience. They will probably give the meditation instructions that introduce you to a new world of understanding the mind. They will probably conduct regular or occasional interviews with you that should help you overcome obstacles to your practice. And you may end up developing such a respect, or attachment, for them that your relationship with them goes on long after the retreat. Their impact on you can be important in a number of ways so you should get to know something about the ways teachers affect us.

Teachers typically claim some kind of authority, usually explicitly, from a traditional lineage. In the world of Zen, for example, teachers usually trace the transmission of the teachings they received all the way back to the Buddha himself. How credible or meaningful this is is another question. And in Theravada traditions it is usually understood that a teacher has trained under one or another renowned master and took up teaching after gaining the master's assent. They might say something like, "My teacher, XYZ, gave me permission to teach." On the other hand, some modern lay meditators have simply gained a large enough following to be generally considered a teacher of good standing.

What do you know about the teacher of your upcoming retreat? Perhaps you've seen a bio, pictures, videos, and lectures on the centre's website or YouTube. Or you may know little more than that they are a monk or nun or layperson. Whatever the case, your assumptions about the teacher may reveal some hidden attitudes that it helps to be aware of. Many people have such extreme expectations of teachers, based on assumptions about Enlightenment, wisdom, and the like, that they have trouble viewing the teacher as a regular human being, and this affects—even undermines—their dealings with the teacher. And at the far end of the scale, people can become downright irrational about teachers, developing a cult-like adoration for everything the teacher has ever said or done.

On the matter of a teacher's achievements, I prefer to start by assuming nothing at all. Teachers almost never explicitly state anything about their meditation attainments, and any such claims on their part or guesses on our part should always be taken with a grain of salt anyway. People can be wrong in their practice self-assessments, and there are major incentives to overstate accomplishments, including profit motive or fame on their part as well as, for our part, finding addictive the notion that our teacher is highly accomplished. Besides, how much does a teacher need to know to be able to get you started? If you are sitting down to learn the piano, you don't need Chopin to teach you finger placement and scales. Perhaps the most suitable mentor is someone a step or two further along than you, because they best understand where you are at and what you need to know to take the next steps. So this line of inquiry isn't likely to lead to any helpful insights.

Or you may find that what makes a good teacher is a deft ability on two fronts at once: balancing a sensitivity to the needs of an individual student with staying true to the traditional framework they are delivering the teachings from. There are teachers who are great at giving helpful theoretical talks to groups, and teachers who connect intuitively with individual students. But a combination of these abilities is special.

On a more general level, people may also view a meditation teacher as a convenient and comforting vessel to pour their guru expectations into. Or a parent-figure to look up to and seek emotional guidance from. They may end up looking for parental-style approval from the teacher and become enamoured or disappointed depending on whether they get that approval. Thanks to Sigmund Freud, we call this Transference, and it's a good idea to be aware of it. Furthermore, if the teacher begins to play that game back to you, known as Counter-Transference, you are likely in an unhealthy and unhelpful relationship. Look for the exit.

On the other hand, some people may find it hard to respect the teacher and his or her advice if they don't conform to preconceived expectations regarding ethnicity, age, gender, or conducting themselves like some kind of serene, supreme being. This is obviously a self-imposed limitation and one we should be careful to let go of.

It's also helpful to spend less time analysing and judging, and more time following the instructions to the letter. I have practised in a range of training environments and not always found a teacher's approach to make sense while on the retreat. For instance, in the Mahasi Sayadaw tradition of Myanmar, teachers are customarily tight-lipped with students. During the interviews, which are usually held around three times a week, the monk prompts the student to describe their meditation experiences. After I reported to the teacher in the official way, they rarely said more than "Keep going" or made a remedial remark or two if it sounded like I was not practising correctly. Probably arising out of my cultural assumptions, I often found it frustrating to receive no feedback or detailed advice. I went into the interview seeking some kind of insight about where my practice was up to and came out none the wiser. I even entertained disruptive thoughts of sceptical doubt. Does the teacher not understand what I'm reporting? Are they new at this and don't know where I'm at? Am I doing something wrong or misunderstanding all of this? When this went on for weeks, it was difficult to stay the course.

Some time passed before I realised such teachers are gently pointing at something while I only see their finger. They were actually intending to be helpful by not filling up my head with too much to think about. It has taken much experience to realise that the "Keep going" teachers are signalling "You are doing just fine; if you keep it up, good things will come." But I was too hot-headed and driven by desire for achievements to see it. I needed verbal pats on the back and hints around achievements in order to feel encouraged. So these days I have a renewed gratitude for those teachers and their reticent brand of wisdom.

Regarding guru expectations, some prominent Western teachers who are aware of the preconceptions students bring to retreats speak of setting out to defuse such unhelpful ideas. They say they deploy expletives or bad jokes or coarse behaviour to help students see them as regular human beings rather than demi-gods to be revered and adored. I once sat through a well-known Western monk teacher's ten-minute excruciatingly detailed saga about going to the toilet! By the end, while the audience gasped for breath from laughing so hard, he had succeeded in destroying any illusions people may have had about him. He was most definitely a regular flesh and blood human being. On the other hand, we should be on our guard about teachers that seek to foster guru adoration.

It's in your own best interests to take a respectful but realistic approach to your teacher. The meditation world has been rocked from time to time by instances of scandalous excesses and abuses by teachers who demanded slavish adherence to their every whim or were put on a pedestal by students. Furthermore, in order to avoid unhealthy relationship dynamics, it's helpful to view the teacher as a subject matter expert who may be able to assist you to improve your meditation practice, but that the help stops there. After all, he or she is only a meditation teacher, not a psychotherapist or a proxy for your parental or religious needs.

To return to the Zen illustration of a teacher pointing to the moon while the students become engrossed in the finger rather than the moon, it is possible to become more focused on the teacher than on what they are there to point out to us. Long after they are gone or you have moved on, there will still only be you and your practice. So you should let the journey be your teacher and guide. By following your instincts to seek out the truth, you will eventually find the guidance you need without falling into attachment to traditions, teachers, doctrines, or dogma. Of course, much gratitude is due to everyone (alive or dead) who helps us along the way, but each of us has to do the work and cannot rely on others or our feelings for others to drive this effort.

CHAPTER EIGHTEEN

Continuity of practice

A common habit among meditators, which you can observe on almost any retreat, is to finish a sitting session, get up from the cushion and go for a wander, or a lie-down, or to read a book, or even to have a chat. Clearly they believe the essence of meditation is in sitting on the cushion and when off the cushion they can drop the practice and go do other things. This is a costly misunderstanding.

Training the mind requires intensity of practice over an extended period. This is why the silent intensive retreat format is by far the most effective way to achieve that training. Outside the retreat there are plenty of distractions, including ones we actively participate in, like addictive device usage, or ones we have little choice about such as commuting to work, and all such activities are detrimental to intensive meditation training.

So when on retreat, we should make the most of the silent, supportive, intensive environment. And this means staying in the meditative practice throughout the day, from waking in the morning to falling asleep at night. Of course, it's very difficult to maintain an unbroken stream of moments in which we are constantly on the job and it's normal to lose the thread of the practice sometimes and fall into daydreaming or in-depth thinking. But we can do our best to keep up consistent awareness of our experiences from moment to moment.

Some meditation methods foster this through detailed instructions to keep up mindful observation of the movements of the body parts, the changes in posture, the mental states that arise and pass away, and so on, at all times throughout the daily schedule. But even in those methods that don't include such instructions, you can still resolve for your own benefit to bring awareness to each and every moment, not allowing the mind to drift off into distracting and potentially disruptive mental states. In concentration-related training, for instance, we should strive to stay with the object of our meditation between sits.

We call this continuity of practice. To keep up the intensity of the practice is to keep pushing the mind along a trajectory of development and advancement. To drop off from that intensity means the mind regresses back down the path you've been pushing it along all this time.

Trite analogy incoming! Imagine that meditation training is like pedalling a bike up a hill. Each moment that you keep the attention where it's meant to be is like a turn of the pedals and a surge onwards up the hill. Sure, occasionally you'll drift off and get lost in thought, which is like taking your feet off the pedals and coming to a stop or even rolling backwards. It's a normal part of the training, but with enough experience this kind of drifting away will become less and less common and therefore your momentum and uphill progress will continue with greater strength.

It makes no sense to invest all that effort hour after hour in the sitting position and then to get up, walk away, and let your mindfulness or concentration degrade back to where you started. It's like pedalling the bike up the hill X metres during the sit, then going away and engaging in distracting activities like scrolling through social media, and the bike rolls back down the same X metres to where your last sit began. Admittedly, practice progress is more nuanced than this, but the principle should be clear.

Let's look in more detail at meditation progress by hours. But please note numbers of hours do not alone determine one's meditation progress. Each meditator brings their own unique mix of strengths and weaknesses, expectations and assumptions, not to mention the role of the teacher and the setting, so every retreat has different outcomes for every meditator. The following numbers are only to prove a general conceptual point.

Mainstream Western acceptance of the benefits of meditation practice first began with the work of American professor of medicine Jon Kabat-Zinn. In the 1970s he developed the eight-week MBSR (Mindfulness-Based Stress Reduction) course which has exploded in popularity and spread across fields of application over the decades. To give you a sense of the scale of the course, it involves attending a two-and-a-half-hour class per week, which consists of various meditation-related activities, and attendees are also expected to complete a daily forty-five-minute meditation session at home. There's also a full day of training during the course. That's around seventy hours of practice over fifty-six days. From that relatively small investment of time, studies have shown enormous benefits for attendees in the areas of focus, awareness, emotional regulation, calmness, and alleviation of stress. See Further Resources for information on scientific studies into the effects of meditation.

Now that all sounds well and good, but we could ask, *If that modest amount of practice can lead to significant developments, how about turning the dial all the way up like the ancients used to do?* On an intensive retreat of ten days at a fairly manageable ten hours per day, that's 100 hours of practice. Or try a one-month retreat at, say twelve hours a day, and that's 360 hours. That's a whole year of one-hour-a-day practice accomplished in only one month! And since continuous practice progress generally compounds, you can see that intensive retreats are the best way to get the benefits of meditation practice and its improvements in mental acuity. (Again, such numbers are only a rough indicator and are not the whole story so please don't count hours as some kind of accomplishment.)

There is a principle underlying all of these details that I have, over the years, taken much encouragement from. Often, we may lose confidence or run into challenging stages in our practice, or we may experience what seem like setbacks. For example, we may find our meditation skills improve day-by-day until we are sitting for longer periods than ever before, able to observe details more precisely and consistently than ever before, and we may experience a sense of thrill at these clear signs of progress. And then the next day trouble begins. Pain quickly arises, the mind does not want to stay put and do the practice, and we end up in a world of struggle and unhappiness. Despite how it sounds, this is a sign of progress in the practice. Think of it like changing up a gear in your car, and the way the engine labours for a moment before catching on and accelerating away. Similarly, our mind may strengthen to a point where it effectively changes gears, and at first it feels like falling back into lower stages of weakness and difficulty. So, whatever happens along the way, a helpful principle to carry with you is this:

As long as you are keeping up the practice,
you are undoubtedly progressing.

If you turn up each day and do what you're meant to do, then whatever you are experiencing is progress. Write that down and take it with you on retreat. This reminder will help you through tough times.

Although the timeframe of a retreat may seem long at the outset, a week or a month does pass and we return to our lives and move on. So there is plenty of time for regret if you have not given 100 per cent effort during every moment of the retreat. If you manage to fit a retreat into your busy life, please be mindful of how valuable that time and opportunity are. After the retreat, you will have what seems like unlimited time to catch up on rest, daydreaming, and social media.

CHAPTER NINETEEN

Sleep time

Retreat centre schedules often allow only about six hours of sleep per night. And this factor alone has put off some people who have contacted me about where to go training. But it's not the obstacle it might seem, because your need for sleep on retreat is normally less than at home.

First, when on retreat you're typically burning a lot less energy than when moving around in daily life, so you'll need less rest. Plus, you'll be surprised to find once your practice has gained momentum, you require a lot less sleep than at home. Mindfulness practice focuses and energises the mind, so the longer you train, the less sleep you need.

On every retreat, I find my need for sleep decreases with the weeks. In the first week, the six or so hours a night can leave me a little sleepy, especially after lunch. But by the second week, I find six hours is plenty of rest. And after a few more weeks, four to five hours becomes sufficient. There was one retreat where my practice was humming along and I was experiencing more and more energy. At the peak of this energetic period, one night I went to bed at 10pm and woke up only two and a half hours later, feeling fully rested and ready to go. I admit it was quite disorientating. Anyway, I got up and sat on the cushion for a while to pass the time until the 3am alarm.

I would encourage you not to worry over the matter of sleep and just see how you adapt with experience. Of course, you might feel a little sleepy in the first few days. But you will find there are ways to cope. One is to make the most of any flexibility in the schedule to take a nap. For example, there is usually a break period following lunch. And on some retreats, each day's first and last sitting sessions are optional so those periods are a great chance to catch up on rest.

Having said all of this, we should recognise what the desire for sleep represents. Ultimately, wanting to lie down and enjoy some time off is caving in to a desire for sensual comfort and is more often than not the result of mental stress. The adjustment to the retreat routine or the climate or food or whatever mental discomforts are arising can drive us to want to zone out, switch off, or shut down. Giving in to these urges just feeds the expectation in future instances that there is a way out. Instead, if we resist these desires to go and rest, we will eventually find we overcome and move beyond them. It's all just a matter of seeing how these things arise.

So don't let the sleep issue put you off. If it were impossible to function on less sleep than normal, retreats would not run in this manner. We'll look again at the topic of energy and pushing through tiredness later on under the Five Hindrances and also under Effort.

CHAPTER TWENTY

Mental health

The relationship between intensive meditation and mental health is a complicated, nuanced one. Intensive meditation practices can trigger challenging responses in people who are affected by mental health issues, especially of the psychiatric variety. And this is why almost all centres encourage people with mental health histories to seek professional advice before attending a retreat. Many centres also warn applicants up front that they do not have the expertise to deal with mental health crises. However, this doesn't stop some people from omitting their mental health issues from the application, which can lead to later trouble.

Please note that meditation training, especially insight practice, is meant to help you see into the underlying reality of your existence, such as that it is impermanent, replete with suffering, and ultimately not the preserve of an unshifting notion of self. But it is not therapy and is not there to solve your psychological struggles, such as emotional patterns from childhood, the effects of past trauma, or the difficulties of life changes. While meditation insights may help you better understand and cope with those psychological matters, they exist in different albeit overlapping spheres of mental training. You might look under the bonnet to see into the operations of your car engine and come to the understanding of why it produces noise and heat, but the car would still have wonky wheel alignment and a broken windscreen. Apologies for the dodgy metaphor, but the intent should be clear.

In the West, meditation is seen as a form of mental health treatment. Sure, at the basic level, simple mindfulness practices can be helpful for mild anxiety, depression, addiction, anger, and the like. It also has obvious benefits in simply granting us time out from a busy or stressful life to go somewhere quiet to sit in stillness. But we should recognise that intensive retreats involve high degrees of mental intensity and pressure that can take us down some unusual rabbit holes. When we observe mental and physical phenomena closely and persistently, we may experience a breaking down of our normal perceptions of stable "reality".

Let's do an experiment together. I hope you're alone in a quiet place or this might elicit some odd looks. Pick any polysyllabic word—try cooking, wandering, quietly, machinery, or anything else you like—then close your eyes and say it out loud to yourself, as fast as you can, over and over. Keep this up non-stop for about one minute, then come back to continue reading.

What did you find?

First, you probably got tongue-tied as the word became garbled and its normal rhythm was lost. Perhaps the word cooking became *googging* or *king-cook*. Second, you should have noticed the more you said it, the more the word devolved into strange sounds devoid of the usual conceptual meaning you would experience when hearing that word in a normal context. When heard once, the word gives rise to an idea, a notion, a concept, in the mind. When heard many times like this, it gradually becomes divorced from those semiotic roots and we begin to experience it for what it really is: sounds. The sense experience has been separated from the concept instinctively trained to arise with it, and you're now in touch with the deeper truth that linguistic concepts arise in our minds via ingrained reactions to sounds.

So too does meditation break down our normal perceptual relationship to our apparent reality. When we watch over and over countless times in close detail the changes in the body and mind that we normally allow to create for us an unquestioned experience of solid, dependable embodiment and consistent, continuous presence, we may begin to feel our relationship to this reality break down. It can be an alarming realisation, and may give rise to anxious reactions, or even trigger psychosis in someone with a pre-existing condition.

The experiences I'm referring to can include but are not limited to the following fairly common selection. It's worth noting that in a clinical context many of these, if persistent, would be deemed symptoms of pathology.

Type	Description	Examples
Disidentification/ Dissociation	Bodily or mental experiences don't accord with who or what we think we are; absence of connection to one's previously solid reality.	Where is my sense of self? Whose arm is this? Who is thinking this?
Derealisation	The feeling one is separated from the world.	The room doesn't look right. I see, hear, and feel things from far away as if through a reversed telescope.
Proprioceptive confusion and disorientation	The signals from the body are garbled and the position of body parts is confused.	My arms feel metres long. My head seems upside down. My legs are beside me, separated from my hips.
Dissolution of boundary between self and other	The feeling we are in other happenings, or events are happening in me.	The sounds coming from outside the room are happening inside my head. Movements in the room are felt happening to my body.
Confused perceptions of space and time	Overlaps between sleep and waking experiences, or absence of a sense of time, or where I currently am.	Am I awake or dreaming? Time seems to have stopped completely. I no longer have any sense of where I am located.

I've had brief encounters with all of these states during training, and in an odd way I usually found them fun. There is a specific stage on the Vipassana meditation journey when signals become garbled and such experiences can occur. Once when doing a long sitting session on the floor of my *kuti* (hut), it suddenly occurred to my perception that my legs were standing straight beneath me. But a couple of hours previously I had sat down cross-legged on a mat on a concrete floor so this didn't make sense. Without opening my eyes, I mentally checked all the details, from the hips down to the toes. I wriggled the toes: yes, they were feeding back messages that they were down there a metre below the floor, pressing into the ground. I tensed the thigh muscles: yes, they definitely felt as if they were standing vertically and holding my weight. The realisation this was a clear instance of proprioceptive confusion made me burst out laughing. I had to suppress the urge to raise my hands and search around for my legs. After some time of observing the sensations coming from the legs that the mind was confused about, I finally had to let go of the illusion and opened my eyes to look down. Sure enough, the legs were crossed beneath me as always, and in that instant the mind's map of the body updated and there was no longer any mismatch.

In case any of the above sounds alarming, these experiences are short-lived and leave us with amused surprise or amazement and do not persist outside the meditation session. In my opinion, they are among the many rewards of intensive training because they reveal to us how flimsy is our grasp on what we see as concrete, bedrock reality. As some meditators like to say, intensive retreats are like extreme sports, but for the mind: they take us far from our comfort zones and comfortable assumptions. They also exert unusual pressure on us. Just as you wouldn't do challenging rock-climbing with a spinal condition, it's best to avoid intensive meditation practices if you have mental health difficulties that can be triggered by these experiences.

If at any time on a retreat you find yourself with shortness of breath, racing of the mind, rapid heartbeat, or other uncomfortable experiences, take a break, relax back, and let go of whatever you're doing. If it doesn't settle down, take a long look out of the window or go for a walk in the grounds. There are no awards for pushing yourself to some kind of breaking point. And if such feelings continue, go have a chat with the teacher. They are likely to have experience with these matters and can give helpful advice. Having said all of this, and to ground this discussion, most people attend retreats without incident.

*　*　*

We should acknowledge that people often seek out intensive meditation training through the experience of some kind of life hardship. And if the ancient stories of the Buddha's life are to be believed, this is precisely what brought him to meditation. Upon realising in the full flush of youth that ageing, sickness, and death were inevitable for all living beings, he chose the uncomplicated life of a homeless seeker, better to search for answers to the fundamental questions that troubled him.

Arguably the Buddha's most significant discovery was that suffering is integral to the experience of the untrained life. This is most obvious to us at difficult times such as the loss of a loved one or facing up to the inevitability of our own demise. But the suffering he was pointing out is not some fleeting mental state that arises in response to intermittent unpleasant or painful inputs. It is the very core of our biological programming and is omnipresent throughout our lives. A deep-seated desire to escape difficulties (such as danger, hunger, rejection) while pursuing comforts (such as food, shelter, emotional connection) is what drives us forward. And this instinct for dissatisfaction has equipped us well for survival. An organism that routinely experiences satisfaction would not make the strenuous effort required to survive and so would quickly become food for another.

In response to this hum of dissatisfaction that runs in the background of our every moment of existence, we have learnt to turn our attention away. And consequently our society's recommended way of life makes us addicted to a barrage of experiences centred on denial, a daily assault on all of the senses at once that takes us away from facing these difficulties with honesty and wisdom. We have all surely seen enough of this life to acknowledge such avoidance simply doesn't work. In fact, looking the other way has the intriguing effect of making problems worse. So breaking away from our habituated responses and facing down these challenging mental states at the core of our psyche may indeed lead us into some deep and powerful experiences. No one should suggest this journey is easy or for the faint of heart. It is not for nothing that a large portion of humanity has for millennia looked in awe upon the Buddha's remarkable breakthroughs. That is a high bar to reach for.

I set all of this down as encouragement if you are unclear about whether your life struggles constitute sufficient psychopathology to preclude you from retreats, or whether the challenges that may occur on a retreat are worth facing. At an ultimate level, there is only suffering and the way to its end. But on a conventional level, there may be mental illness that prohibits someone from the training, and if you have such a history, you should speak to a trusted specialist to find out about options, including lighter approaches.

CHAPTER TWENTY-ONE

Other meditators

It's a fascinating reflection of the complexities of our minds that many of us go on retreat to confront or deal with difficulties we perceive in our daily lives, such as relationship challenges, personality shortcomings, and the like. And yet when on retreat some of us can end up in rather unwholesome involvement with others, as if bringing those very difficulties into the retreat with us, or simply failing to see them arise right before our eyes. In the worst cases, these difficulties can derail a person's retreat.

One variety of this is to develop anger or resentment towards other meditators. As part of intensive meditation practice, we might endure periods of agitation or ill will, which we could end up projecting onto the people around us, especially anyone we find off-putting in any slight way. They may be making noise or dressing in an unusual way or flouting the rules of the centre. We need to be very much on our guard about these developments in our minds because they can become a major source of disruption in our own practice as well as even escalate to the level of open hostilities, dragging the other person into our dramas, not to mention onlookers. Being fully aware it's happening is the best way to overcome it.

At the other end of the spectrum are romantic attachments. In the rather restrained environs of the retreat, finding another retreatant powerfully attractive can be as big a source of trouble as the resentment mentioned above. It's possible to work up stories in our mind about the other person until they become the sole focus of our attention. They seem so serene, or so calm, or so damned good-looking in that headwear or that shawl, that we can't stop watching them and thinking about them. We may resolve to speak to them on the day of departure and may spend endless hours mulling over what to say and do to achieve the hallowed goal of getting their contact details.

Again, this is usually a result of difficult experiences arising in the practice and giving in to this pressure will undermine our meditation. More often than not, once off the retreat we'll find the feelings rapidly fade, daily life reasserts itself, and we'll be amazed at how much those fantasies consumed our thoughts. Take it as another valuable demonstration of the power of the mind to generate its own convincing reality out of fleeting, passing conditions. But mostly just be aware if it begins to happen and then you can strive to let go of such thoughts. Try moving your sitting equipment over to the other end of the hall, or come and go by a different door. It won't benefit your practice in any way to get so entangled.

We may also find we look around and compare ourselves to other meditators. Let's say you are struggling along in a difficult sitting session and you open one eye and look at your neighbours. They may be sitting firmly and silently, and you begin to feel demoralised because you're convinced they are all doing so well while you're struggling to stay with the practice. There are two things to learn here. First is that everyone struggles with intensive meditation practice. Not all in the same way at the same time, but no one has a consistently easy run of it. Second is that criticising ourselves is a common habit learned from many years of competitive striving in our normal lives, and it is not at all helpful. Comparing ourselves to others is one of the most certain ways to feel worse. So bring what the Buddha called wise attention to where your mind goes, to ensure it doesn't get caught up in such self-defeating routines.

Some people find *Metta* (loving-kindness) meditation a helpful solution that softens the mind and makes us more accepting and compassionate. It can be practised a little each morning to remind us of all the things we are grateful for, such as good health, the supportive conditions of the meditation centre's facilities, the teacher's efforts to guide us, our family's support, and so on. Your teacher may be willing to give you some advice on *Metta* practice, or else see Further Resources.

In the final analysis, if self-improvement is one of your goals on a retreat, try practising compassion and loving-kindness towards the very people you find yourself among while there. How you cope with them is the first test of your newfound self-awareness.

CHAPTER TWENTY-TWO

Leaving retreat

A final note before we close this section. After all our hard work of training the mind while on retreat, we typically depart the centre with little forethought for what we'll face outside. Weeks or even months spent in a silent, peaceful atmosphere, as well as existing in a powerfully concentrated state, can leave us shocked when running up against the jarring, noisy, fast-moving world beyond the gate. The longer the retreat, the more this can be an issue. And the further from home you are, the more you might have to deal with.

Some retreat centres encourage chatting and socialising on the final day before departure to help us acclimatise back into human society. Others don't. I would recommend making time after the retreat for at least a couple of days of downtime before trying to go back to work or arriving back in a busy family setting. If you've gone overseas for your retreat, then fitting in some travel in the area should be easy. Try a short trek, a weekend on a quiet beach, or a few days of wandering among temples and museums.

The first day out after each of the multi-month retreats I undertook over the years, I went for a walk in the area of the monastery. A flood of odd experiences quickly struck me, like seeing dogs and children for the first time in what seemed like years. And frequent eye contact and interactions with countless strangers. I found it easier to wander the quieter parts of town until I adapted again to the cacophony of sensory engagement that is normal street life.

There is one more aspect to emerging from a retreat. For some of us, a meditation retreat can open up novel and powerful experiences that cast our lives in a new light, open new horizons for us to consider, or give us new perspectives on our relationships, lifestyles, or careers. To leave the retreat emboldened with this new mindset and run up against the routine of our pre-retreat lives could create a storm of complications for us, and also for our partners, families, workmates, and friends.

For example, consider a person who leaves a retreat after some kind of mind-blowing insights, now newly invested with overt spiritual energy and convinced their job or relationship is holding them back from walking the path to some notion of ultimate freedom. They may decide it's time to pack up their life and go hit the road with a backpack to find themselves. While a retreat can be a chance to see our lives in a new and sometimes insightful light, it can also create unrealistic short-term outlooks that prove damaging to our livelihoods and relationships.

Be sure to pay attention to such inclinations as you depart and head home, and consider putting any such major breaks with the past on the back burner while waiting to see if these new thoughts and beliefs last: that is, if they continue to yield helpful insights and improvements in the coming weeks and months. We will come back around to this important topic in more detail with a discussion of the controversial notion of the Dark Night.

INTERLUDE 2

Insight meditation instructions

This exercise begins similarly to the first exercise. Let's sit down in a comfortable posture in a quiet place.

The objective:

> To observe closely the most predominant experience while it is happening.

We do this by bringing awareness to the experience which most grabs our attention and stating a one-word label for the experience we're focusing on. We use the -ing form of the verb to indicate it is currently happening and state it in our mind, not out loud. We'll begin with the largest and most consistent movement in the body during meditation: the rising and falling of the abdomen.

After settling into your sitting position, the breath in the abdomen is likely to become predominant in your field of attention. Notice the upward and outward movement of the abdomen as the breath comes in, labelling it *rising*, and the downward and inward movement as the breath goes out, labelling it *falling*. Remember: we should never manipulate or force the breath in any way. We are only observing.

So to reiterate, as the belly rises when the breath comes in, we state in our mind *rising*, and as it sinks, *falling*. When we discover the mind is wandering and thinking, our attention has left the rising and falling so we must bring attention to the new object of awareness—thoughts in the mind—and label this *thinking*. When it fades and the breath becomes predominant again, we return to the observation of the rising and falling of the abdomen. We may notice a sound, so we observe this experience and label it *hearing*. We may notice a tingling sensation in our foot, so we observe it and label it *tingling*. You can also label it *feeling* or whatever other word suits. In fact, the choice of words is up to you and is not important in itself.

The key to this method is to be *labelling and observing while the experience is happening*. So we observe the rising sensation of the abdomen and simultaneously label it *rising*. Then we observe the falling sensation of the abdomen and simultaneously label it *falling*.

If at first you find it difficult to locate clear sensations of the breath rising and falling, place your hand on your belly and notice how it rises and falls, labelling each movement. When you're ready, you can return your hand to its resting place then bring the attention back to the abdomen. Be sure to label the movements of the hand from and to its resting place. *Moving, placing,* etc.

Note that it is not sufficient just to notice the abdomen has begun rising, label it, and then have a daydream until the falling begins some seconds later. The attention must stay on the observed experience from its beginning, throughout its duration, all the way to its last moment, and all the while labelling it. If this means drawing out the label slowly to fill the time or repeating it a couple of times or just stating it at the start then watching the rest of the movement: these details are up to you to decide. Again, the important thing is to label it and observe it throughout its entire duration. *Rising, falling, rising, falling ...*

After some time in the sitting posture, you may notice a pain arising in, say, the middle of your back. If the pain draws your attention away from the breath, then bring your awareness to the pain and label it *hurting*. Keep observing it and keep labelling it. If it persists, see if your attention can notice finer details such as the precise location, edges, and changes of the painful sensations. Eventually it may go away or change or soften. At some point, other sensations will become more predominant and your attention will go there, labelling all the while. If the pain continues and you decide to move the body, be sure to label it all, including *shifting* the posture, *rubbing* the spot, *thinking* about it, *feeling* annoyed by it, *wanting* it to go away, and so on.

> *Everything in our entire field of experience that comes to the foreground of our attention should be observed and labelled.*

Be patient, it will take time to build a vocabulary for all the countless activities you will notice in the body and the mind. This method is a little more challenging than the first one so give it some time. The benefits take a while to become apparent. You may notice you can practise this method off the cushion as well. When you finish the session, be sure to move slowly and keep labelling: *moving, standing, turning, walking, looking, lifting, drinking,* etc.

Summary. Focus the attention on the most predominant sensory or mental event in your field of awareness. Label that event with a word while watching it closely. When the attention moves elsewhere, apply the attention and labelling to the new event. You should find the attention eventually rests with the rising and falling of the abdomen.

Advanced tip. The challenge is to achieve precise and clear observation, so zoom the attention in and seek to observe details within details. Observe the beginning, middle, and end of each movement. Also, after some practice you may find there are too many things being noticed to label them all. You may notice constantly changing states in the mind and sensations arising all around the body at a pace too fast to take stock of. Some meditators report frustration at this stage. But the good news is this is a sign your practice has strengthened and deepened. Feel free to drop the mental labelling and just keep observing everything the best you can, including any agitation or excitement or other reactions that arise. These are all part of the process. Keep going!

PART III

MEDITATION: PHYSICAL

Whatever harm an enemy may do to an enemy, or a hater to a hater, an ill-directed mind inflicts on oneself greater harm.
Neither mother, father, nor any other relative can do one greater good than one's own well-directed mind.

—*Dhammapada verses 42–43*,
translation by Buddharakkhita Thera

CHAPTER TWENTY-THREE

Morality

Of the three aspects of Buddhist training, morality (*sīla* in Pali) is presented first. The second is concentration (*samādhi*) and the third is wisdom (*paññā*). They are to be developed sequentially on the understanding that morality supports the development of concentration, which supports the development of wisdom, which brings us back around to morality. The detailed schema for developing these three areas of training is known as the Noble Eightfold Path. It's an interesting topic in its own right, but is beyond the scope of this book so feel free to investigate it more in Further Resources.

A feature of the modern approach to meditation training is to see it as a standalone activity, independent of and unrelated to practices that are apparently extraneous, like morality. But the traditional approach has never seen it this way. It helps to think of the goal of Buddhist practice as the purification of the mind, cleansing it of a lifetime's worth of flawed and faulty thinking and actions. To do this effectively calls for more than just sitting and observing the breath or some other object. It involves a broader campaign across multiple fronts at once, to ensure the bad habits have nowhere to go to hide. For example, when one focuses exclusively on meditation practice and ignores morality, the mental defilements can persist in such activities as transgressing the basic boundaries of harming, taking inappropriate liberties with others and their property, and using unpleasant language. This will stall a meditator's progress as surely as if they were practising incorrectly. On the other hand, a wise meditator, who is keenly aware of the danger of crossing those boundaries and the costly effects that can have on the development of their concentration and wisdom, will respect the holistic framework in which the mind progresses towards refinement, purification, and liberation. If you're from outside a traditional Buddhist culture, I sincerely and respectfully encourage you to invest time to investigate how the observance of morality can support your meditation practice, rather than breezing over it like a superfluous formality, which is how it is presented in some modern settings.

At traditional retreats, you will likely be invited to take precepts or vows at the beginning. The first five precepts are the basic requisites of morality, covering off the boundaries across which harm begins. They are not just applied to meditators on retreat but are also usually expected of laypeople in Buddhist communities. They cover:

- Avoiding killing or harming other beings
- Avoiding taking what is not given
- Avoiding sexual misconduct
- Avoiding wrong speech (lying; harsh speech; criticising and dividing others; and idle chatter)
- Avoiding intoxicants (they lower our inhibitions regarding the other four).

Consider the importance of these precepts. If you found yourself among a community of people who sincerely strove to live by these rules, how would you feel? For example, to be among people who you can see making an effort not to harm insects or mosquitoes, never touching what is not explicitly offered to them, and speaking gently and considerately, you would probably find yourself free of doubts about whether they would also treat you, your body, and your possessions with the same regard.

That's one obvious reason to cultivate such behaviours among a community such as the group of people sharing a retreat centre. But there's another important one, according to the Buddha's teachings on liberation. When we sit and pay attention to each moment as it unfolds, inevitably our minds wander to thinking. That thinking is very often dominated by remorse and guilt around things we may have done wrong or just neglected to take proper care of. Especially the feelings of others.

In fact, it's usually the first big lesson we discover about ourselves on a retreat: much of our mental activity involves how bad or doubtful we feel about the past, ourselves, or our future possibilities for happiness based on our past record. And in response we work up stories to defend ourselves against self-reproach by re-running events or conversations over and over *ad nauseam*, in which we seek to absolve our consciences of our past misdeeds or failures. Seeing this and realising how unhappy it makes us feel, we are better positioned to see the importance of avoiding doing things in the present that will store up future unhappiness for us.

And this is where morality or virtuous conduct comes in. To bring deliberate attention to avoiding behaviours and actions that will create further difficulties in the future is to begin the process of cultivating a mind free from remorse, guilt, and other sources of misery and restlessness. This is really the crux of the Buddha's frequent exhortations to bring virtuous intentions to bear in our daily behaviour. A mind free from self-doubt, self-criticism, and fear of reproach or punishment is a mind that easily settles into calm and concentrated states. And you might recall the second area of meditative development is concentration.

It always strikes me in the first few days at a monastery that my mind becomes distinctly quieter and calmer. Settling into a simple routine of eating what is given, sleeping only as much as is needed, performing wholesome chores like sweeping, and not having to get entangled in complex decision-making trade-offs, there is a sense of a clearing out of clutter and obstacles. Our morality training is also helped by sticking to commitments. Getting up on time, attending all the scheduled sessions, keeping ourselves and our quarters clean. These can contribute to a purified mind, all the more suitable for calm, steady observation exercises.

Let's revisit the point I've made before:

> *The attitude we bring to the practice is as important as the practice itself.*

With the goal of clear-sighted awareness and calm, focused concentration, we are far better positioned if we have developed a way of life surrounding the practice which is free from self-reproach, guilt, shame, and fear of loss or failure. And this is why the importance of morality, or virtuous conduct, cannot be overstated.

Be that as it may, devoting time to morality training can be a hard sell in our easy-come easy-go age. A person who strives to purify their moral conduct to help improve their meditation might not see the benefits of their efforts right away, and it is so much the case these days that people are accustomed to lightning-fast results. In these times where a tap on a device can bring food to our door within minutes or products within hours, or a dictated question can give us an instant canned answer on any obscure matter, or the press of a button puts us in live video contact with people around the world, to spend weeks or months exclusively engaged in a demanding activity with what may look like intangible results seems a massively disproportionate investment.

It's easy to see it this way, but it is also a mistaken attitude. Developing one's virtuous conduct not only improves our meditation progress, in our daily life we will also see the difference in the increased trust and respect that people have in us, as well as our own self-acceptance and happiness. While hard to quantify in the short term, the ultimate value of these outcomes is also hard to overstate.

To help explain the process of improving one's morality, one teacher spoke of the metaphor of seeds. Imagine you're planting a seed every time you perform an action, no matter how big or small. If the action is unwholesome or harmful, the seed you just planted cannot but give rise to an unpleasant fruit some time down the track, in the form of doubts and regrets. And of course, wholesome or helpful actions and their seeds will give rise to pleasant fruits someday, in the form of confidence and calmness. This is a basic law of the universe as old as time.

While it's true that the greatest benefits of observing the morality of our behaviour can take years to develop, like the flourishing of a garden, it's also true that you can experience benefits within a retreat. To adhere to the rules and ensure we never do another being any intentional harm, never use what we don't have a right to, avoid sexual inappropriateness, speak kindly if we speak at all, and abstain from alcohol and other intoxicating substances, is to ensure a mental attitude free of conflict, self-criticism, and doubt about our behaviour and suitability for the practice right there and then. On a related level, committing ourselves wholeheartedly to the schedule, the meditation method, and the consistent dedicated effort required is another way to improve the clarity and regret-free state of our minds.

On a retreat, when we experience the improved clarity and calmness these commitments can give us, it also tends to inspire us to bring those precepts and wholesome behaviours home with us after the retreat. And in the end, this might prove to be the biggest benefit of our training. That's no small achievement!

CHAPTER TWENTY-FOUR

Aches and pains

Let's face it: no one likes pain. Least of all the persistent kind that seems to have no purpose or point. And it's a fact of meditation retreats that along the way you will confront a variety of aches and pains as well as your mental reactions to them.

If you ever try to sit completely still, it won't take long before you notice discomfort arising in the body. It might be a point of pain in the middle of your back, or a dull ache on the underside of your thigh, or you might even be surprised by a sting appearing in a random place like your wrist. In our normal unmindful daily lives outside meditation practice, we've become so accustomed to these tiny experiences that we don't think about them. We just automatically shift the posture or move a limb to make them go away, usually not even consciously noticing any of this process occurring. Then another source of discomfort appears somewhere else and we go through the same autopilot response. It goes on all day and our minds never achieve a completely settled state.

In meditation, because you shouldn't shift and move every time you encounter an uncomfortable sensation, you'll find yourself coming into full contact with these aches and pains. In some cases, the pain may seem so unpleasant that there's no choice but to shift. Feeling compelled to break our meditation routine and shift frequently can be dispiriting and make us doubt whether we are any good at meditation or whether the retreat was a good idea after all.

First, the good news is it's completely normal because everyone goes through this. Second, it gets more manageable and with enough practice it can be overcome. Third, the not so good news is the only way from first to second is to sit with it. There are no shortcuts on the meditation journey!

At first, we may fall into the trap of misinterpreting what the pain means. We may dredge up stories of past injuries and poor posture and so on, and arrive at the conclusion we only need to find a more comfortable way to sit, or use a painkiller, or sleep it off, and then we'll settle into a magically painless posture. In fact, there's something quite different happening inside so it's important to let go of these stories as they may end up undermining our resolve to push on with the routine.

The key to understanding aches and pains in meditation is to recognise their true source: *an agitated mind*. We human beings aren't used to staying completely still for long periods so it can be an unsettling experience at first. As you sit on the cushion, stationary and silent, the mind begins to perceive facets of its experience that it normally doesn't see, and they can be difficult to come to terms with. Facets like dissatisfaction with how things are in the moment, with the scope of one's desires versus the reality of one's existence, with frustration at the forces that seem to keep us from fulfilling our desires, and so on. They may appear with full force or instead lurk at the edge of our awareness. Either way, the experience of these mental states is unpleasant and we go for the habitual response: distraction.

Even the pleasant moments experienced in meditation, such as may arise in concentration practice, are eventually observed to be ending or unattainable in any lasting sense and this may lead to disappointment. The result—whether pleasant or unpleasant—is the mind doesn't want to see this any longer, it has a little tantrum, and a distracting discomfort arises somewhere in the body. Throughout our lives it's proven to be the perfect remedy to the unpleasantness of exposure to unwanted states because we would normally shift the body, thereby breaking the concentration and freeing the mind from awareness of that unpleasantness, albeit only until the next unpleasant experience arises. Repeat this cycle over and over and you see why most people shift, fidget, and look around frequently in daily life. Add in a mobile device and you can also see why people have that constant need to fidget with the phone and tap and scroll their way out of the present moment. But in meditation this frequent shifting and fidgeting is not an option. With time, the mental discomfort can intensify and so does the physical reactivity. Hence why that point of pain in the back or the thigh may persist and not go away.

But, someone might counter, *I really do have a sensitive knee from a past injury so when the pain comes up I know it's the old injury recurring.*

Are you sure it's the old injury flaring up again, or is it the mind generating pain there because it's a past source of discomfort, one that is easily accepted as a pain that needs to be remedied with a shift? The entire leg, from the hips down to the toes, contains dozens of muscles, tendons, and ligaments, and any combination of them can be gently tensed just enough that with the passing of time a pain begins to arise there. That initial small tension is an easy achievement for a mind preoccupied with discontent or agitation.

One teacher I've trained with responds to such complaints about pain during sitting with a simple question. "What happens to the pain when you get up from the meditation?" The response is always, "It disappears." The teacher smiles and waits for the student to get the point.

If you ever have the privilege of training alongside seasoned monks and nuns, notice how still and silent they are when sitting. It's hard to believe how stationary someone can be, hour after hour. The years of intensive training have settled their minds so well that there is little or none of the agitation that gives rise to the aches and pains. This is a powerful outcome that people who persevere with their practice will notice and enjoy.

Like tiredness, aches and pains can be overcome by sitting patiently with them, not by caving in and going for a break or a lie-down. With enough training the mind learns that uncomfortable mental states can be coped with in equanimity. And they eventually cease causing the bodily discomfort we have spent our lives caving in to. This explains one of the instructions you're likely to encounter on your retreat: to stay sitting till the end of the session, even if you have to adjust the body sometimes. The mind will eventually discover the vital lesson that uncomfortable states can be overcome, but only by not caving in as we always have, every day of our lives until now.

Please note this is not a call to subject oneself to tremendous suffering as part of some heroic quest. In the early stages it is OK to let go and shift when needed. Gradually we get stronger and clearer about how to see through the challenges of longer sits. It is also true that many hours of sitting can result in genuine body fatigue such as joint pains. Experience will show you the difference.

With enough consistent training, a meditator arrives at a stage where there is often no discomfort whatsoever in the body. When on retreat, you will discover your sitting sessions are gradually getting longer and your stamina for strongly focused sitting grows. Eventually it is even possible that you may sit for several hours at a time without major posture adjustments. These experiences will change your meditation life because they are irrefutable evidence that sufficient practice can profoundly transform the relationship between the body and the mind, as well as our perceptions of suffering and contentment.

Until that stage, there are some helpful ways to cope with the difficulties that are likely to turn up. Some meditation methods offer ways to examine aches and pains, while others don't. Whatever the case, if the pain is becoming a bother, break your observation of the official object—say, the breath—and bring the attention to the pain.

If you just observe the pain and think about how unpleasant it is, you'll probably find the mental suffering increases. Instead, let's be a scientist and take a close look at its physical attributes. Where is it located exactly? What area does it cover? Is it only on the surface or does it go deep inside? What is its nature: stinging, aching, stabbing, burning, grinding, rubbing, cutting, etc? Is it constant or does it throb, pulse, or even move around? And if you watch it closely over a period of, say, a minute or two, does it fade away, move around, or get worse?

Here's a spoiler. The very act of bringing this much close examination to the experience of the pain may be enough to make it fade away or morph into something less troubling. Of course, this result is not something to go looking for or expecting of your practice, it's just what may happen if the conditions are there. It's not easy and it's not guaranteed every time. But there's no satisfaction like the first time you dive into the experience of a pain somewhere in the body only to see it fade away until it's either gone completely or has morphed into a dull sensation that is no longer painful.

If the pain persists, even under extended examination, it's time to adjust the posture. When you do this, bring calmness to the task, slowly lifting, moving, and placing the limbs, rather than haphazardly flinging the body parts around to escape the pain. Again, this is about easing the mind into experiencing its true moment-to-moment reality, not running from it.

If pain continues to arise, some teachers recommend standing next to your cushion for a while until the blood flow has returned and the pain has faded away. Or you can go outside to do walking meditation. Again, there should be some kind of instructions about this or the teacher should be happy to give advice.

All of the above is to encourage you to dig deep and overcome one of the early impediments to meditation progress. But it's also important to note that in extreme cases we may find ourselves sitting in a posture that is not suitable for our body. This can result in straining ligaments or joints, even causing an injury. In these cases, of course you should change your posture or move to a different sitting situation to alleviate the strain. Eventually you will know whether this is a legitimate strain on the body or just the mind's trickery to get you to shift and break concentration yet again.

CHAPTER TWENTY-FIVE

Postures

The early Buddhist texts detail four main meditation postures, and today these four are still in use. My friend Becky will demonstrate.

Walking

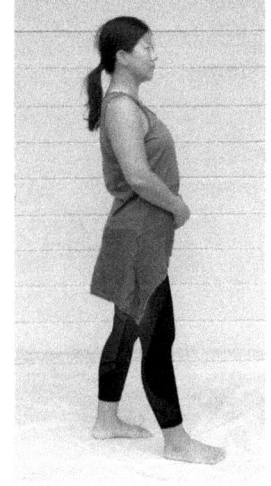

As you might expect, this involves placing one foot in front of the other while keeping attention on observing the details of the movements. Walking meditation is taught in some traditions as an extremely slow-moving practice, allowing for deep mindfulness and concentration, and in others as brisk striding. In some you are encouraged to walk naturally, while in others there are strict ways to hold the body and the hands. You are likely to find some people casually use it to relax and loosen up the limbs between long sitting sessions, while for others it is a formal, focused mindfulness practice. One major tradition advises against doing walking meditation during a retreat, while for another major tradition it is an integral part of the practice. As you can see, there are many ways that walking meditation may be part of the retreat training routine. Your teacher is sure to give advice on this. See Interlude 3 for instructions.

Walking meditation is the most energetic of the four postures, and is usually advised for when one is feeling sleepy.

Standing

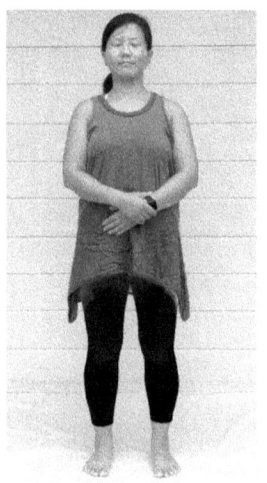

This is not so common and it's possible to attend an entire retreat and not give it a try. Standing is the second most energetic posture so teachers usually only recommend it as an antidote to sleepiness when sitting. If standing for long enough, it is easy to lose your balance, so place the feet shoulder-width apart and keep the eyes slightly open. Leaning lightly against a wall or railing is a good way to avoid getting disoriented. After settling into this posture, it is possible to bring the attention to the breath at the nose or abdomen just as in sitting meditation. It is also possible to bring attention to other sensations such as the feet pressing down on the floor or the clasping of the hands. Just remember: in order to avoid toppling over, keep up the overall bodily awareness.

Sitting

Sitting is less energetic than the previous two postures so it's where sleepiness can catch us, especially in the early stages of a retreat. But since it is the core practice of pretty much all traditions, it is where our training focus should be. Note the principles of a good sitting posture: pelvis tilted slightly forward to allow a gentle concave curve in the lower back, head up straight, and shoulders square. It helps to place the hands somewhere that does not leave you with tension in the arms, so resting the hands on the upper thighs or crossed ankles is usually most comfortable. Below we will look at further options for how to sit.

Lying down

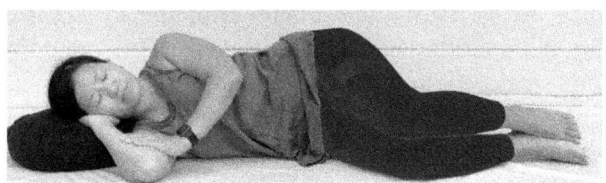

This posture is rarely recommended by teachers and never in the early stages of one's practice. The reason is obvious: when we lie down and close our eyes, we are programmed by a lifetime of experience to fall asleep.

The Buddha himself is reputed to have practised and recommended a lying down position called the Lion Posture. Lie on the right side with the right hand under the head, the left arm lying along your side or resting wherever comfortable, and the feet resting one on top of the other. The name comes from the way a lion's rear feet do this when lying down. Note that lying on the left side puts pressure on the heart and can result in discomfort, so it is not advised.

This is the lowest energy posture and will probably result in sleepiness. At the advanced levels of practice when you are experiencing plenty of mental energy, especially when doing many consecutive hours of sitting, lying down can be a useful way to rest the body because the mind won't be able to get drowsy. Also, for a meditator at any level, it's a great way to go to sleep at the end of a day of practice because you can continue the meditation until losing consciousness. Give it a try!

Sitting options

It seems everyone quickly settles on a posture that becomes their main way of sitting. So you will find what works best for you fairly early on. It pays to experiment a little to know what's available, but beware of the following.

First, you should understand there is no such thing as a perfect posture in which you can sit forever without discomfort. It's the nature of our bodies that we experience the beginnings of aches, pains, discomfort, or restlessness within minutes of sitting down. The key to making a sitting posture work for you is to understand that you're ultimately training the mind to adapt to a new relationship between mind and body, rather than looking for a perfect posture that never hurts.

Second, you're likely to find that most postures feel good enough when you first adopt them and it's only after some time, maybe a half-hour or so, that the limitations become clear. So take some time to check how each one works for you.

Third, sitting posture is intimately personal so it doesn't help to follow or copy others. Instead, experiment with the methods below to find one that allows you to sit for, say, a half-hour without much pain. That would be a good start from which to build your stamina.

Having said that, in at least one tradition—the Zen school of Japan, China, Korea, and Vietnam—you are typically expected to sit in one version or another of the Lotus posture with the hands joined and thumbs pressed together. In a different example, people from a yoga training background like to rest their hands palms up on the knees with thumb and finger joined. And at the other end of the scale is what you'll encounter in South-East Asia, especially Myanmar, where the attitude seems to be that as long as you sit upright and still, no one minds what you do with your hands or legs. I'm a fan of this kind of pragmatism. If it works, it works.

A fundamental reason for developing an effective sitting posture is to immobilise the body, which leads to neutralising of sensory activity. Eventually the range of activities to observe, or to be distracted by, will decrease until one's attention naturally comes to rest on the predominant object of the meditation. So any posture which involves unnecessary movement or tension of any degree is going to be less effective. Let's look at the details.

Any good sitting position calls for the spine to be upright. This usually requires a slight forward tilt of the pelvis creating a gentle concave curve in the small of the back, while the upper half of the back should be straight and the shoulders relaxed but upright to avoid hunching over to the front. It is possible to find a way to sit like this without strain or unnecessary tension. On the other hand, you can tell fatigue has set in when your body reverts to a degraded posture such as slumped shoulders, hunched spine, or head tilting down.

Once you've settled on a position (the main ones are detailed below), bring attention to the way the abdomen tends to expand and contract with the breath, rather than the ribcage moving up and down as you might normally experience when moving around in active daily life.

This is the key to good meditation practice as the body should move as little as possible, and gentle abdominal breathing tends to support this, whereas the ribcage expanding and contracting causes the rest of the upper body to move as well. Try it now. If you breathe deep and long with your chest, you will notice your shoulders move and your arms and hands may shift slightly too. When you instead allow the breath to settle deep down in the abdominal cavity, moving forward when inhaling and sinking back in when exhaling, no other parts of the body are affected. This allows the settling of the body and the stilling of its normal flurry of sensations so the mind can come to rest.

The following postures are listed in a rough order of difficulty from most to least challenging. That is, the first one, the Full Lotus, tends to be difficult or impossible for most people. The last one, the chair, tends to be the easiest for most people. That said, be careful of inclining towards easy solutions. Sitting with your back upright but unsupported is the most important aspect of the sitting posture because it positions the spine vertically and opens the respiratory system for unhindered breathing. It also helps to keep the mind alert and energetic.

Full lotus

In this position, a meditator usually sits flat on the floor without a cushion. It's like sitting cross-legged except each foot rests on top of the opposite thigh instead of underneath the shins. Think of a pretzel. This posture requires a special degree of flexibility and openness in the hips. For those who can sustain it, the position seems to be stable and long-lasting. It's also the posture that was probably in vogue with the ancients, including the Buddha and his disciples, so for some people it has a special significance.

Half lotus

This is almost the same as above, but while one foot rests on top of the opposite thigh, the remaining foot just rests underneath. It has similar advantages to the Full Lotus but can be done with a little less flexibility.

Quarter lotus

Also based on the previous posture, the meditator rests the lower portion of one leg on top of the lower portion of the other. It's a very common position as it doesn't require much flexibility. Normally a cushion or other support is used under the buttocks, and the knees either press down on the mat or are also supported by some kind of padding. The only drawback for some people is that nerves can be constricted and the legs can become numb.

Burmese position

I find this a useful posture when the above Quarter Lotus becomes uncomfortable, as it takes only a simple manoeuvre to shift into. The lower leg remains where it is, and the upper leg is pushed forward to rest on the mat parallel to the lower leg. A small shift in the pelvis is also required to allow the upper leg to move forward. The benefit is that both legs are free of anything pressing down on them and causing numbness. The drawback is that it can be awkward for the pelvis and upper legs.

Cross-legged

This is the standard in South-East Asian meditation settings. Sitting flat on the floor or on a thin mat, the meditator just crosses the legs and rests the hands on the thighs or lower legs. It seems to work for a lot of other people, but I find it difficult to keep the back upright as the inclination is to slouch forward. So I avoid this one. But see how it works for you. The fact this posture can be used anywhere without support makes it handy.

Kneeling with cushion

Again, some people seem able to do this while the rest of us cannot maintain it for long. The knees are parted a little on the floor in front of the body and the hands rest on the thighs. This is a handy posture as you can move to it from any other cushion-based posture.

Kneeling with bench

This is the same but with a bench under the buttocks to lift the upper body off the lower legs. Benches are becoming increasingly common as more people discover how comfortable this posture is. In my experience, one benefit is the straight-up spine that it naturally encourages. I recommend borrowing a bench and seeing how it works for you, especially if the other postures are difficult. Folding benches are available these days, which pack well for travel to a retreat. A variation on the bench is placing a tall cushion between the lower legs to support the upper body weight.

Chair

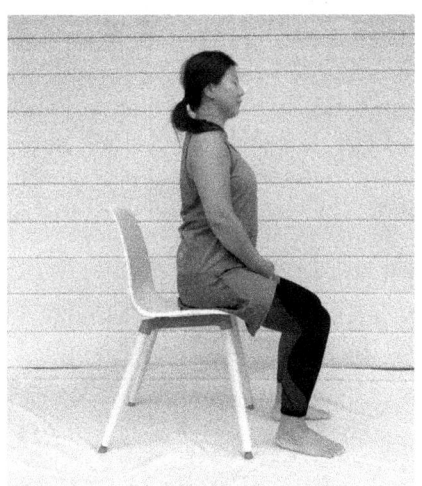

Slightly controversial, this is the last of our sitting options. In a traditional setting, chairs are rarely used for serious meditation, except in the case of old or unwell people. On the other hand, Westerners are increasingly choosing the chair as their go-to posture since many find sitting on the floor to be a struggle. In some centres, meditators are discouraged from using a chair in the absence of a serious medical condition, while in other centres many people use them freely.

There are a few things to consider about resorting to the regular use of a chair. First, leaning into the back of a chair undermines the straight-up spinal position that is required for long, relaxed breathing and supporting the mind with a strong physical base for energetic training. A lounging body can also signal to the mind that it's OK to slack off and get sleepy. Second, even the comfort of a chair can deteriorate over time as the mind becomes weary and generates discomfort in novel ways throughout the body. So it's not a fail-safe solution. Third, if you come to rely on a chair but then find yourself in a setting where you are refused the use of one, the adjustment to another posture may be a struggle.

If you use a chair at all, be sure to position yourself to the front and keep the spine upright away from the backrest. Or you can use a cushion at your lower back to position yourself away from the back of the chair.

As a result of some years of experience of numerous postures I can say using a chair as your main sitting method will eventually be a bad idea. Please do persevere with the above postures first and, if it feels necessary, resort to a chair only in cases of the most severe fatigue, such as in the final sit of the evening. Most of the above sitting postures are commonly used because they provide a solid, stable base that supports strong meditation practice. Lounging back or resting on a chair rarely achieves this. So a good rule of thumb is to avoid chairs unless you're advanced in age or suffer from a medical condition so severe that it makes floor-sitting impossible.

One more point is that traditional Asian Buddhist etiquette teaches that it is impolite to sit or stand above a teacher or monastic person, so when they are present, please do sit on the floor if at all possible.

CHAPTER TWENTY-SIX

Samatha vs. Vipassana

Throughout the two-and-a-half-millennium history of Buddhist meditation, there has been a lot of debate around the details of methods. There is a body of early texts discussing aspects of the approaches to meditation and, with the passing of the centuries, new texts arose commenting on the early texts. Hence, their categorisation as "commentaries". The history of Buddhist texts is colourful, complicated, and fascinating, but we won't go into it here. Suffice to say, the main source of debate is around the position that there are two separate strands of meditation practice: *Samatha* and *Vipassana*. I should start out by stressing the earliest texts mostly do not treat them as distinct practices, and their complete separation came as a later development.

So while it is possible to see this entire topic as a phantom of sectarianism, there is an ongoing debate that prompts a common question from newcomers: *What's the difference between these two?* The subtext of the question is usually: *Which one should I be doing?*

Let's start with the meaning of the words.

Samatha (pronounced sa-mat-ha) is a Pali word (Sanskrit: śamatha) commonly understood to mean tranquility and refers to the calmness of mind arrived at when one achieves concentration. Within this form of practice is *jhāna* (Sanskrit: *dhyāna*) meditation, where *jhānas* are discrete states of concentration that the meditator can navigate through.

Vipassana (pronounced vi-pas-sana) is a Pali word (Sanskrit: *vipaśyanā*) commonly understood to mean insight, in the sense of intuitive knowledge. So, as one observes details of physical and mental experience, insights occur in a specific order that lead to liberative breakthroughs. In Western countries, Vipassana is often rendered as insight meditation.

The debate about which method one should practise has raged since time immemorial, with different factions supporting the practice of one or the other only, or both separately or both together. One might ask: *Why is there a debate? And why does the difference matter?* These are great questions to be guided by as they keep you open to learning your way through the complexities. Otherwise, the destination you arrive at will have a lot to do with preconceptions or doctrinal biases.

The story goes that the Buddha, when he was just a young man seeking answers, started out training in what has become known as Samatha. He is reported to have mastered the *jhānas*, the states of concentration that ascend through degrees of refinement up to the eighth *jhāna*. Despite mastering these, he had failed to attain the final release he was seeking. So he headed off into the wild and joined with other seekers to delve into ascetic practices of depriving the body of sustenance and comfort. Such practices were done in those days with the goal of training the mind to accept suffering and thereby overcome it. As you might guess, it didn't work and he was left chastened by these failures. Eventually he decided on a different route, which became known as the Middle Way: the letting go of extremes. Despite how reasonable it sounds to us, legend says his abandoning of the extremes of starvation and deprivation for the more practical way of eating and resting adequately earned him the derision and rejection of his fellow ascetics. Off he went alone to find his way to the final release.

Although the early texts are somewhat unclear on the details of how he meditated after that, it's probable he went back to practising *jhānas* (Samatha) and brought investigation (Vipassana) to his experiences. This development gave rise to insights about the mind and its delusions, which culminated in his final awakening, known in English as Enlightenment.

Looked at like that, you might assume the correct pathway to follow to that ultimate realisation is to start off with Samatha practice, follow it up with some Vipassana, and *voila*, the gates of *Nibbāna* (Sanskrit:

Nirvāṇa) will open for you. And this is the basic position of one of the largest meditation schools, established by Pa-Auk Sayadaw (born 1934) of Myanmar. (Sayadaw is Burmese for master or teacher.) He teaches Samatha first, then Vipassana investigation as a later stage, taking as a basis a combination of both the earliest texts and a later commentary known as the *Visuddhimagga*.

But that's not the end.

The other side of the debate says that, while Samatha practice is good to have in one's bag of meditation skills, it's immensely time-consuming and not at all essential. It is argued that Vipassana alone is enough to take a meditator all the way to the highest attainments of the Buddhist path. The inference here seems to be that the Buddha's early training in Samatha was an unnecessary sidetrack. You can imagine this is an unpopular view among the other faction above. The insight-only route is known as "dry Vipassana", and the testimony of countless living people who have trained in this method seems to support the claim it is a quick and efficient route. However, as you might guess, shortcuts come at a cost. The main tradition on this side is known as the Mahasi method, named after Mahasi Sayadaw (1904–1982) of Myanmar. After rising to prominence as a scholar early in his monastic career, he decided to learn meditation instead and went off to train with an old master. From the combination of that experience and his prodigious textual knowledge, he devised the quite simple instructions that have become known as the method bearing his name. When applied carefully and persistently, these instructions do indeed lead to rapid and fascinating progress.

So, what's still to understand?

This is where it gets complicated and can depend upon a meditator's training background as to what they think from here on. As usual with complicated matters, neither side is entirely right or wrong, and the ultimate understanding may have something to do with their interdependence.

Within pure Vipassana practice, especially once one has made some progress along the path of insight, the lack of concentration abilities becomes increasingly obvious. It's true that within Vipassana training one can develop concentration abilities along the way, but it's not a deliberate or focused part of the training and so may take a while for this skill set to become appropriately strengthened through indirect effort. It's reasonable that some people may not develop these skills and never progress beyond a certain stage. The genius move of Mahasi Sayadaw is that he managed to distil a shortened, simplified, and somewhat direct path to realisation for modern meditators. So while his method is largely viewed as highly effective, it came at the price of some valuable and foundational skills.

To understand the next point, we should note that the path of pure Vipassana training can be a gruelling experience for most people, covering a range of territory that includes some dark and stressful stages. By contrast, it's well-known that in Samatha practice one can experience blissful states and one's practice can become a generally comfortable journey. So for some people, these concentration states may be addictive and condition them to expect comfort on the cushion, making Vipassana practice so challenging as to be prohibitive. Having said that, a counter-view is that a solid base of Samatha practice can carry one more smoothly through the rocky stages of the Vipassana path.

Since you're reading this book, I'll wager you value what I think, at least a little bit. First, the Samatha-first path for some can be so long that a meditator may not progress to the stage of developing Vipassana to a meaningful extent. I am not recommending shortcuts for their own sake, but instead I recognise people have worldly limitations. In my opinion, most people have only so much stamina for developing their meditation through long bouts of intensive training before the need for building careers, having families, and preparing for retirement takes over. Or if they have left the training until the later stages of life, they have only so many years of strength and stamina left. On the other hand, Vipassana-only people report attaining important breakthroughs after mere months or a few short years of regular training. But there's a catch: those same people often later report getting bogged down where Samatha skills are called for. Of course, they only have to work on those before continuing on, so it's not a dead end.

OK, so that was a bit non-committal. That's because the real answer is less about which one to do or whether one is superior, and more about what you want to achieve. If you're looking for a daily practice to help you get along in life, then Samatha is a good way to go. It is relatively well-suited to practising in a daily life situation and can be relaxing and healing. Look for any kind of concentration practice to take you in this direction.

If you're on a more soteriological path of seeking after the ideals of liberation and release from suffering, there is the Samatha-Vipassana path of schools like Pa-Auk, or the Vipassana-only path of schools like Mahasi.

This whole discussion is to a large extent a false dichotomy. Some modern meditation schools treat these two strands as if they are separate or mutually exclusive, whereas an examination of the earliest texts shows they were intended to work in tandem, like the two wings of a bird. See Further Resources.

Sooner or later, whichever of the paths you follow, you're likely to come around to needing some aspect of the other. Furthermore, these days there are methods available to train in which do not conform to either of these two main strands. So at the early stages of your practice, I'd advise not being too concerned but instead to dive in and train as diligently as you can at whatever method is available to you. "Cosmopolitan" meditators can attest to the fact that time spent training in the purification of the mind helps you develop the mental faculties in a general sense, so there's no such thing as wasting time, whatever the method.

CHAPTER TWENTY-SEVEN

Restraint of the senses

Reining in the senses is an area of meditation training that deserves attention and can have a major impact on your practice.

In our daily lives, and resulting from a lifetime of habit-forming behaviour, we've become the slaves of our senses, drawing our attention outwards into the world around us, looking here and there, listening to this and that, revelling in tastes and smells and physical sensations, as well as the meanderings and ruminations of the mind. (Note that in Buddhist terms, there are six senses: the five physical ones plus the mind, which is considered an organ that senses mental activity.)

You will notice this more than ever after a retreat, the fact the mind constantly wanders to thoughts that inspire and enrage, to sights that titillate as well as annoy, and tuning in to sounds ranging from the pleasant to the irritating: the whole gamut, regardless of whether it's enjoyable or not. We seem programmed to revel in sensual engagement with the world, no matter the content, as if it enjoins us to life itself. Well, in the traditional Buddhist critique, this is precisely what's going on and is the source of our inability to sit still, bring attention inwards, and observe what's there beneath it all.

Whatever the meditation method or tradition, they all involve bringing the mind to one or another object of observation and then seeking to keep the attention there. To do this well requires letting go of the mind's habit of flying off to investigate whatever sense impression is knocking on our sense doors. "Look at that colourful bird, and the voices over there discussing something, and oh, that memory of my last holiday in the sun!" Sensual activity like this is a constant source of distraction, but the good news is that meditation helps us see it for what it is and let it go. (Note that in Buddhist terms "sensual" simply refers to the wide gamut of varieties of sensory enjoyment.)

While on retreat, we should work on developing the habit of lowering the head and the eyes so the visual field shows only the floor in front of us. Start by noticing how powerful is the temptation to raise the head and feast the eyes on what is going on around you. A person walks through the corner of your field of vision and immediately you'll notice the intention in the mind to direct the eyes over there and take in who it is. If you give in to that desire, you might also notice the zooming in of attention to check out the person's particulars. Once you've begun to notice this kind of urge, you can reason with it and overcome it.

At the start of a retreat, I often chuckle at my habitual reactivity when doing this, noticing how desperately the mind wants to engage with and know everything, mostly things that have no relevance to me or my situation. Passing by a garden, a brightly coloured rose is noticed in the corner of my view and arising suddenly is a strong desire to see and roam the eyes over its subtle and intricate form. Or there's that colourful sunset sky and how badly I want to raise the head and take it all in. In daily life we see no harm in such micro-indulgences. But when training the mind, we need to be aware at all times of how our attention is directed.

While the eyes tend to be our dominant sense, the same distractions occur via the ears. Notice how quickly the mind tunes in to whatever sounds it picks up from the surroundings. The teacher and a student are chatting over there by the admin office and, after weeks without conversation with others, my ears are suddenly aflame with the desire to catch the words and know more about what they're discussing. Such instances are a good opportunity to smile at my foolhardiness and then bring the attention back to the present moment.

The same goes for the body's touch, the tongue, and the nose, although in daily activities these senses tend to be less distracting than the eyes and ears.

Finally, there's the mind: the most distracting of all due to the sheer infinity of possible topics, places, memories, fantasies, and speculations it can get entangled in. And note how the physical senses can trigger the mind and vice versa. The eyes or ears notice something, then the mind catches on to that topic and runs with it. Seconds or minutes can fly by as the mind continues to ruminate about whatever the eyes or ears picked up on. Or there is a thought and then the eyes and ears prick up to follow through on the implications of the thought in the world around us.

The valuable lesson to be learned here is that we are always in search of sensory stimulation with the ultimate aim of taking us away from moment-to-moment engagement with our actual existence. At first when we restrain our senses, we may experience a painful reactivity—an unhappy mind or aches and tension in the body—and we may misinterpret this as a sign that restraint causes pain. But in fact, ceasing to revel in sensual distractions brings us more into touch with the underlying suffering that is there all along, is central to the human condition, and is the impetus for the pursuit of sensory indulgences. So restraining the senses not only helps our meditation development, it can show us something vital about our existential predicament.

On my first retreat I didn't fully understand the importance of this area of the practice. Each day after lunch I had a routine of wandering around the grounds, inspecting flowers and insects and other people. One day I even wandered over to the boundary wall, stood up on my toes and surveyed the surrounding countryside, gawking at workers and passers-by and what they were doing. The following day at my interview with the teacher, he told me he'd seen me looking over the wall and counselled me to "restrain the senses". Deeply embarrassed at being caught out, I asked how and he gave some advice. After leaving the interview, I did exactly as instructed and went back to the meditation, determined to try whatever would help avoid any future embarrassment. Two days later at the next interview, when I reported on the whole new range of meditative experiences observed, the teacher was very pleased, reminding me that restraining the senses and bringing the attention back to the objects of observation had given a powerful boost to my lagging mindfulness. I've been committed ever since to bringing attention to how the unrestrained senses can degrade the intensity of our focus, concentration, and mindfulness.

Reining in the senses pertains also to issues discussed elsewhere about device usage, reading books, keeping a journal, judging one's fellow meditators, and speculating and doubting about the practice and the teacher's methods. All of these habitual addictive behaviours undermine the intensity of our practice and should be overcome with full effort.

CHAPTER TWENTY-EIGHT

Anicca

Pronounced *a-nee-cha*, this is a Pali word (Sanskrit: *anitya*) typically translated into English as impermanence, sometimes as change. Impermanence is a satisfactory choice and is often heard in Buddhist meditation circles because it is the first of the Three Marks of Existence: the three aspects of reality present in all instances of existence. Together they are *anicca* (impermanence), *dukkha* (suffering), and *anattā* (non-self).

There's a lot to say on this trio, but I've singled out *anicca* for a closer look at how we can investigate and understand the myriad Buddhist concepts that we will encounter on our journey. It's also a helpful introduction to why Buddhist inquiry is not merely intellectual philosophy, but requires examination of our actual moment-to-moment experience in order to fully grasp what it has to show us.

Please note this chapter is best undertaken when you have the time and patience to explore the meditation-related exercises that follow. Feel free to come back once you're relaxing at home.

* * *

When you first hear of the teachings around *anicca*—that everything is impermanent—you would be forgiven for thinking it's kind of obvious and not particularly profound. We all grasp intellectually that everything changes and ages. We see it happen to ourselves in many ways: we are no longer the children we once were; our hair and nails get longer and need trimming; and eventually everyone's hair turns white or falls out and our bodies sag and weaken. We also see our houses suffer wear and tear and deteriorate: that's why we need to paint and fix them often. And we notice how our cities and neighbourhoods evolve over time. So it's not particularly illuminating for a spiritual teaching to point this out to us. But let's take a microscope and go in for a closer look at what the Buddha was really getting at.

Yes, changes at a large scale are obviously part of how the world works. It was summer not long ago and it'll be summer again in a while. It's evening and soon it'll be morning, then it'll be afternoon, then evening again. But have you also noticed how our internal world changes? Have you noticed how once upon a time you cared little about something, and now you feel very strongly when you reflect on the same issue? Or have you noticed how you were angry about something recently, and today when you bring up the memory of it you barely register any reaction at all? And given a week or two you will probably need someone to prompt you just to recall it ever happened.

All of this is *anicca*. The examples are endless.

To get another look at this, let's zoom in on our physical experience. Bring attention to your body as you read this. As you are sitting or lying down, do you feel the movement of your heartbeat or notice the undulations of the torso with the breath? Put your attention there for some moments and feel the movements. Resist the temptation to rush through this chapter and instead just keep watching until the movements and changes have been fully noticed.

Did you fidget or blink or adjust any part of your body or posture just now? Notice the awareness of a change in the body, not only in the area where the change happened, but in the surrounding areas, as well as in your overall bodily state. One moment something was like that, now it is like this. In a few moments it will be different again.

How about your visual sense? Your eyes are running from left to right along the lines of text. Do you notice that no matter how carefully you sit still or hold the book or device, your visual scene is shifting ever so slightly? Even if only by millimetres. So notice that no matter how steady you think you are, your eyes are never taking in *exactly the same scene* in two consecutive moments. The same goes for what you're hearing all around: the sounds arriving at your ears are always changing. Try it right now. In no two instances is the complex cornucopia of aural stimulation striking your ears the same.

Now bring your attention to the parts of your body resting on whatever surface you're currently sitting or lying on. Are the sensations there completely still and unchanging, like dull blocks, or can you detect tiny shifts, movements, or vibrations? You may need to zoom your attention in to the level of pinpricks of sensation. One moment the squashing of the left buttock is clearly perceived as an area of fuzzy, buzzing sensations, then it's faded and now the sensations on the underneath of the right thigh have become predominant. Next the fine vibratory sensations around the elbow resting on something are clearest. Stop reading here and check on your own experience.

All of these discoveries show us that even our physical experience is a constantly shifting array of inputs and signals. *Anicca*. No two moments are entirely the same. You could say everything is *constantly changing*: a delightful Buddhist oxymoron!

Having examined the current state or perception of the body, join me in an experiment. Stand up and take three steps in any direction. Go on, do it. Then keep reading.

Now pay attention again to all those areas of the body you just examined moments ago. Do they feel the same? Is the same weight or tension occurring in all the same places? Or have those zones vanished and now there are entirely new areas of sensation and tension and pressure and weight? How about your feet and legs?

It might occur to us to wonder if this is the same body that was sitting just moments ago. Of course, common sense tells us it is. But how about your *experience* of the body? Is it exactly the same experience? Not at all. Not even close. Consider how much more so this body has changed since an hour ago, or yesterday, or last week. We inhabit a world constructed out of default concepts that obscure our actual experience of reality under layers upon layers of unquestioned assumptions. Sure, it's convenient to do so, but it also separates us from a more accurate and awakened experience of our existence.

When we zoom in and make a close examination, we are likely to notice vibrations, tingling, and the appearance and disappearance of tiny instances of sensation that make up the bigger impression of a body part or posture. I like to view this coming and going of countless tiny points of sensory input like the pixels rapidly flickering on a detuned TV screen. Notice how no sooner has a pixel appeared than it vanishes before you can properly observe it. This is what our physical sensations are like at any given moment when observed in fine enough detail.

Now that we've had a good look at our physical experience, let's turn our attention to the mind. Throughout all of the earlier investigations, the mind has also been going through similarly minute and rapid changes. Let's take this sentence: between starting it and finishing it, you might detect a different perspective, mood, assumption, or flow of background ideas running in your stream of consciousness. At the very least, you will have noticed you started the sentence unaware of how it would end, but now you know. So if you consider that at any moment *you* as a psychological entity are the conglomeration of the contents of your consciousness, and since those contents have been updated or changed in the past few seconds, we could even say you are no longer exactly the same person who started reading this paragraph.

Anicca ... anicca ... anicca. No two moments are exactly the same. And in no two moments are we exactly the same.

So what can we learn from all of this investigation? We have seen that our perception of our physical and mental experiences consists of a rapidly shifting, flickering, arising, changing, and disappearing storm of sensory inputs. So in fact our awareness of being here right now is nothing more than a seething mass of impermanent signals arising in every single living, breathing moment, so quickly and so briefly as to be barely there at all. When looked at closely enough, there is nothing in our entire experience that is not rapidly changing and immediately vanishing, including the mind with which we are doing the observing. Again, no two moments are exactly the same, in here or out there, and in no two moments are we exactly the same.

If you've absorbed that and are ready for more, let's investigate the rapidity of these changes. Zoom in again. Where you see the arising and changing of sensations—whether it's the buttocks on the sofa or the hands holding the book or the flickering of lingering signals on the retina—investigate how long a moment of sensory experience is. If you think it's, say, a second, then lean in and see how many micro-moments of tiny changes can be observed between each larger instance of change that you think is happening per second. Perhaps now you can notice there are several slivers of experience within each second. Go closer, what's between those slivers? Can you perceive even tinier moments of shifting, changing, arising, and passing *anicca*?

This is not an easy degree of observation to get into or to keep up, so persevere with it when you have the time and some peace and quiet.

When we observe this constant and rapid change in every aspect of our experience, we discover that our original preconceived understanding of our existence is flawed. We saw ourselves as a solid, fixed, stable, unchanging platform from which to work with reality in a way that is dependable, certain, and predictable. Instead, the true nature of our experience is revealed to us by observing what is actually happening within our body and mind. My experience of being a me in a here and a now is actually not a coherent and solid thing. No philosophical concepts are needed. By observing our own experience, we simply become aware of this underlying truth.

You'll also notice if you now turn your attention to the TV or social media, or get busy dealing with work matters, the atomistic awareness of your moment-to-moment experience will evaporate and all the prior assumptions will flow back in to fill the old spaces in the mind. This is why removing ourselves to an environment free of distractions is vital for meditation practice.

The above meditative investigation goes to the very core of what we think we are and what we think this existence right now is made of. If anything about this exercise feels unsettling, then reflect on the fact that none of it is new. It has been happening in every moment of our existence since we were born. It is *how* we exist. So it cannot in and of itself be bad or wrong. It just is. Everything after that is conceptualising: that is, we add layers of abstractions and beliefs onto it.

Of course, this constantly changing experience, while not in itself good or bad, does have a lot to do with the suffering we endure at the core of the human condition. And you may recall the second of the three marks of existence is *dukkha* (suffering). As you can see, there is no end to this rabbit hole of investigation. The closer you go, the more you see, and the closer you go again. Welcome to the fascinating world of insight meditation without even attending a retreat!

CHAPTER TWENTY-NINE

The meditation hall

In virtually all meditation training environments, the meditation hall (sometimes known as a Dhamma Hall) is the centre of activity and purpose so it tends to be the largest or most central structure. It's usually spacious with a wide open floor space. It may have meditation equipment such as mats and cushions placed throughout or stacked at the side. There is usually a Buddha statue and decorations at the front, depending on the tradition or cultural environment.

Meditation halls also tend to be well lit either by windows or lights and may be breezy or else cooled by fans or air conditioning. In some cold climates it may be heated or at least closed in. Further details vary, but there may be TV screens for recorded lectures, a PA sound system, clocks, portraits of the founder, a podium at the front, and a break-room and bathrooms attached. And finally, depending on the climate, there may be cables or hooks overhead for suspending individual mosquito nets.

One thing all meditation halls have in common is they are subdued and peaceful environments. Apart from lectures (known in some places as Dhamma Talks) that may be live or broadcast on an audio-visual system, you should find the hall a solemn place of peace and quiet or else intense, silent mass training. In most centres you're required to do all or most of your sitting sessions inside the hall, so you will become very familiar with all of its details. And in some centres there may be the added option of sitting in your room or in other areas of the centre such as individual cells.

In most places there is a general unspoken etiquette in the hall. First is to remove footwear to avoid soiling the floor. Second is to bow to the Buddha statue, meaning one kneels on the floor and touches the hands and forehead to the floor three times. This is usually done on entering and leaving the hall, but may depend on the tradition or cultural environment. For guidance, just watch what the seasoned practitioners do. Remember bowing is optional in most places. On a related note, if the teacher is a monk or nun, it is also customary to bow to them in the same manner when attending and leaving one of their talks in the hall. Again, if you're uncomfortable about this, it's rare that anyone pays attention to what you do.

A major point of etiquette is to respect the quiet of the hall by keeping the noise of your movements and activities to a minimum. This means walking slowly and quietly, and positioning yourself on your cushion or other sitting equipment with careful quiet movements. It also means not bringing into the hall unnecessary gear that could end up causing noise. This includes jackets, water bottles, notebooks, clocks and watches that beep or ring, plastic bags that rustle, and so on. Of course, talking is absolutely not on. You'll get the idea once you're there.

Being aware of how we disrupt others in the silence of the meditation hall is especially important because, at certain stages in meditation training, we can experience a surge of agitated mental and bodily states, which can make us take action to relieve the tension we're experiencing. On a retreat, you may see a person caught in the throes of such challenging experiences moving around the hall opening windows or closing doors or changing the air-conditioning settings, apparently with no regard for anyone else in the room. Simply knowing such things can overtake us in the depths of intensive practice should be enough to spot it in ourselves when it arises.

Finally, when treated with respect and reverence, the meditation hall can serve as a place that supports all of us in developing the determination and dedication for quality meditation training.

CHAPTER THIRTY

Exercising

Especially for people with a yoga background, the desire to fit in some form of exercise while on retreat can be strong. But some traditions and centres strictly forbid such activities, especially in and around the meditation hall. The reasons range from avoiding distraction from one's own practice, to stopping people distracting others by carrying out exercise routines around the grounds of the centre. Mostly these admonitions are made with the best intentions to foster a focused and dedicated training environment. Imagine people jogging around the grounds or doing yoga postures in the meditation hall. The injunction also probably has something to do with the Hindu origins of yoga and the Buddhist origins of the meditation centre.

Having said that, if you want to fit in a simple stretching routine or exercise session in the privacy of your room, I would advocate for it due to my past experience. On my first long retreat, I got so absorbed into the practice that my desire for food shrank day by day until I was eating only a small serving at each meal. I also did no exercise whatsoever. It's important to note meditation centres usually don't have mirrors, and when we are bundled up in winter clothes, we may have no idea how our body is faring. When I emerged from the centre three months later, I was shocked to discover a skeletal appearance and a weight loss of 12kg. My limbs had shrivelled so much that lifting my suitcase onto the airport scales was a struggle. It took some months of exercise and eating more wholesomely to recover. If I had kept up a basic exercise routine, I may have had more appetite and emerged in a better physical state.

If you wish to take up a basic exercise routine, be aware of the mind's desire for distraction and keep the workout to a minimum. It's also less disruptive to the practice to bring mindfulness to these exercises, paying attention to the movement of limbs, the stretching sensations, the nature of the breath, and the like. You could do laps up and down a flight of stairs or around a remote corner of the gardens. Or you could do star jumps, push-ups, sit-ups, and squats in your room. You can tailor these workouts to your circumstances by increasing or decreasing the strain. For example, you can do light push-ups by placing your hands on a chair instead of the floor. Or you can hold an object like a water bottle on your head during sit-ups to increase the strain and reduce the number of repetitions. And of course, there's the whole range of yoga and pilates exercises available that should be manageable inside your room.

I find the best time of day for a brief retreat workout is just before a shower, because we are about to be disturbed by the routine of washing and changing clothes anyway.

In the end, it's important not to lose sight of the primary reason for being there and stay focused on the meditation practice. There is a balance a long-term retreatant needs to strike to protect bodily health while not undermining the meditation practice. With experience you'll find ways to make this work. Besides, on a short retreat of only ten days or two weeks, exercise isn't really necessary.

CHAPTER THIRTY-ONE

Daily practice post-retreat

A common concern that crops up when people see the end of their retreat looming is how to maintain everything they've learned and gained during the retreat after they return home. It's an important question and it arises out of your growing commitment to the practice. So bravo! To decide to go on a retreat is the first commitment. The second is to turn up and submit to the training regimen. The third is to push on through the challenging meditation sessions, hour after hour, day after day. Even month after month in some cases. But the final level of commitment tends only to grab our attention when we're leaving the retreat: *What next? How do I keep up the practice?*

For people who already had a daily practice routine prior to the retreat, it isn't such a big deal. It may just require locking in more time each day.

For those coming out of their first meditation retreat, to manage to keep up at least one one-hour sitting session per day could require a big change in the conduct of daily life. The first and main challenge is the other people in our lives. We may have a spouse or children or parents or housemates. And if none of them are meditators, gaining their buy-in and acceptance of this time we need each day to be left alone in silence may be asking a lot. It helps to sit down with them after the retreat and explain how important it is to you to keep up the practice. And as is often stated in the meditation world, the people closest to us usually see most starkly the benefits of our practice. So they may also be the most supportive.

Next we should determine the time of day that will best suit our practice needs. I personally find that going to bed a little early, say 9pm, and getting up at 4am, gives me plenty of time to carry out my morning exercise and meditation routine without disturbing anyone or anyone disturbing me. But if you're not a morning person, you might want to arrange a time slot before bed. Or maybe the hour after breakfast or before lunch, or upon arriving home from work. Whatever works for you.

It's important to be realistic and pragmatic about this because committing to something that isn't going to work will end up being an exercise in disappointment and possibly even self-directed frustration. For example, the later in the day I try to sit down and meditate, the less likely it is to happen. There's less pressure to pack loads of things into each hour at 5am as there is at 5pm. To miss sessions may be demoralising and you'll lose the desire to keep going.

When training at anything, a useful principle is to do slightly less each day than you feel you can manage. That way you will always want to come back to it rather than exhaust the passion. So instead of pushing for two hours each day and causing yourself some disappointment if you can't live up to this, try two half-hour sessions and allow the ardour for further practice to grow those sessions longer and longer.

One meditation tradition ends its retreats with advice on this very matter, including the exhortation to keep up a sit in the morning and another in the evening. This is a noble goal and is reasonable if you live alone without a demanding lifestyle.

For others, modern society's demands to make "productive" use of our time can make it tough to take an hour or two to sit silently and apparently "do nothing". The pressures on us to address the more pressing real-life concerns with every moment of our days will sooner or later overwhelm our meditation goals. We need to remind ourselves that meditation typically helps set us up to cope better with the stresses and demands of daily life and is therefore fundamental to the success of the other areas of life. Just like physical exercise is crucial to our physical well-being. I find reading quality books and listening to good podcasts about meditation help keep me eager to continue the practice. See Further Resources for ideas.

Another way we can fit in more daily practice is to strive to maintain awareness throughout the day, no matter what we're engaged in doing. Bring attention to the experience of eating, of showering, of rushing to catch the train, of meeting with friends, of agitated reactions to work challenges, of simply being alert and present in each moment. This kind of continuous mindfulness throughout the day helps to support our conventional sitting practice. Some meditators also find novel ways to fit in more meditation time throughout their day, such as while riding on a bus or the train, or sitting in the break-room at work, or while waiting for a meeting or class to begin. For me, when going to bed in the evening and finding I'm not quite ready to fall asleep, it can be a great time to practise by bringing attention to the breath or body sensations. There's no limit to how we can work the practice into our daily lives.

Despite all of these encouragements to keep up the practice, it's typically the case that on retreat we're able to achieve much stronger mindfulness and concentration than at home in the midst of our daily routine. So let's go easy on ourselves and not seek to relive the experiences that are mostly only possible on retreat. The intensive and supportive environment of the retreat centre, surrounded by like-minded folks silently practising and a teacher regularly advising us, simply cannot be maintained in the busy world outside the retreat.

On a final note, let me point out that while our meditation practice does benefit from intensity of training such as we get on retreat, it also compounds over time from simply keeping it up a little each day. The rewards will be seen on a future retreat. Consider going on a retreat a year from now: it will make a difference on that retreat whether you kept up one to two hours of sitting each day or none at all. So do strive to work a practice session into your daily routine as soon as you return home. It all adds up!

INTERLUDE 3

Walking meditation instructions

This practice can be a beginner exercise or an advanced technique, depending on how you do it. You should do walking meditation in a space where you can walk at least five metres in one direction then turn around and walk back. Do this over and over for however long you want, but note it should be done extremely slowly. Compared to sitting, this is a fairly energetic form of meditation so it is helpful when you feel sleepy or when you start meditating after a meal.

Like the above insight practice, we should label everything we observe during walking meditation. We can advance in stages. In the first stage, we can walk at a moderate pace, labelling *stepping, stepping,* or *walking, walking,* or *right, left, right, left.* Label the movement as soon as you are aware it has begun and observe it all the way to the end. Aim to be precise.

When we feel the first stage is well-developed, we can move on. Now we label each step in two parts. As the foot begins to move up and away from the ground, we label *lifting*. As the foot descends from its highest point, we label *placing*. Again, the terms are up to you. *Raising* and *dropping* are also OK. Remember to observe closely the sensations that make up the experience of the lifting and the placing. Zoom in and label and observe each movement right at the moment it begins, following it through until the very moment it ends.

In the third and final level of this practice, we label each step in three stages. Same as above, except once the foot is off the ground, we add in an intermediate label, *moving*, for the forward shifting movement of the foot. When this movement is complete and the foot begins to fall towards the floor, we label *placing*. We now have *lifting, moving, placing* as the three stages of each step. Feel free to walk very slowly. The slower you walk, the more detail you can observe, and the less overwhelmed you will feel. And continue the labelling as you turn around to walk back along your route. *Lifting, turning, placing.*

Summary. Walk very slowly, bringing attention to the lifting, moving, and placing of each step. Strive to observe and label each stage of the movement from its very first moment all the way to the final moment, over and over.

Advanced tip. When you feel confident in the third stage described above, focus your attention on watching the finest detail of each stage. Zoom your attention in and look for the tiniest sliver of a moment when the foot begins to move off the ground. Then observe every detail of its lifting movement all the way until you notice the forward movement has begun and label this *moving*, also watching it all the way. When the foot begins to descend, strive to be present there at the very place and in the very moment when it changed. Try to stay present and observe every sub-moment of each of the three stages. The finer the detail you can observe, the stronger your practice.

PART IV

MEDITATION: MENTAL

The only true freedom is freedom from the heart's desires, and the only true happiness this way lies.
—Matt Johnson, singer/songwriter of The The

CHAPTER THIRTY-TWO

Effort

Effort is so central to the practice of meditation that the word has spawned its own special usages. "Over-efforting" means pushing too hard. "Effortless effort" is when the practice has so much momentum that it seems to race along of its own accord with no input required.

In the meditation context, effort comes from the Pali term *viriya* (Sanskrit: *vīrya*), also translated as vigour, energy, and exertion. If any of this sounds familiar, it might be because of the English word virility, meaning strength or energy, which comes from the Latin *vīrīlis*, which comes from who knows where, but I'm guessing this and many other words were shared across the region from northern India to the Mediterranean through the centuries.

The concept of effort is much discussed in the old texts and modern teachers also spend a lot of time discoursing on it. The reason is simple: meditation begins with and is sustained by effort. It requires effort to resolve to meditate, and it takes effort to sit down and begin doing it. More effort is required to bring attention to an object. And effort is called for over and over again to repeatedly bring the attention back after it has wandered. And finally, even more effort is needed to push on day after day and ascend to the heights that meditation training can take us to.

Effort is all about intention. When we are energised to attend to meditation practice out of wholesome intentions, such as to overcome suffering, we position ourselves best for what is to come. On the other hand, if we treat meditation as an obstacle to overcome or treat progress as a goal worthy of an aggressive, egoistic pursuit, we can find ourselves straining, pushing, and striving in ways that undermine our practice. This is what we mean by over-efforting. I recall in the early days of my practice that I would strive so hard for meditation progress that sweat would break out on my temples, and stiffness and tightness would arise in the shoulders, the neck, down the back, and in the legs. All very unpleasant and unhelpful.

Remember this point of wisdom mentioned throughout the book:

The attitude we bring to the practice is as important as the practice itself.

The wrong intention can undermine our efforts as surely as making no effort at all.

If you're a fan of classic martial arts movies, you may have seen the motif of the young firebrand who seeks out a renowned master and implores the old man to train him in deadly fighting techniques. Let's paraphrase the typical exchange. The old master responds to his pleas, "OK, that'll take about ten years." The young man, eager to vanquish his enemies as soon as possible, preferably right away, explodes, "That's too long! I'll work twice as hard!" To which the master says, "OK, then it'll take twenty years." The young man is apoplectic, and pleads, "I'll go without sleep, I'll do whatever it takes!" With the calm of a sage, the master replies, "OK, then it'll take thirty years."

These scenes always result in the humbling of the young antagonist, who submits to the master's instructions, culminating some time later in his attaining both fighting skills and the wisdom to know how to use them judiciously.

As comical as those exchanges seem, they highlight a powerful and inescapable logic one encounters when training the mind. The core of the journey is a gradual process of unfolding, revealing, and letting go into new perspectives. To seek to force that process to suit one's self-centred, greed-driven priorities is to doom the whole enterprise from the outset. The moral of the story? One must bring the right amount of effort to meditation, but no more.

The good news for newcomers is that, in the beginning stages, too little effort is a bigger risk than too much. Every ounce of effort you can bring to your first retreat is likely to be helpful. I'm referring to the effort of getting out of bed on time, keeping to the schedule, continually reminding yourself to stick to the instructions, and overcoming daydreams, doubts, and boredom.

Nevertheless, sometimes over-efforting occurs. For instance, to find clear sensations of the air around our nostrils, we may resort to forcing the breath in and out to increase the vividness of the sensations. A common experience for some meditators is to feel the breath is only happening because of their efforts to make it come in and go out, and so they experience great anxiety at the thought of forgetting to breathe!

This is obviously not going to happen, but it's an example of how wrapped up we can become in unhelpful approaches. If you find yourself struggling like this, let go of the practice, relax, and sit back. Open your eyes and look around, count up to ten then down again, and so on. Forcing the meditation like that is definitely not good practice and anything you can do to bring yourself back to a place of calm and relaxed observation will be beneficial.

In the section on the Five Hindrances, we look at the two pairs of obstacles known as Sloth and Torpor, and Restlessness and Worry. The key to understanding them is how our effort can cause one or the other. If we push and strive too hard, we can end up in restlessness. And if we don't apply enough energy, we can end up in sleepiness. Achieving the right balance will come with experience, but it's a good start just to notice when one or the other is happening and be aware of what that says about our level of effort.

Finally, there are advanced stages of practice in which any degree of effort can be counterproductive. It's wonderful to arrive at such a point in the meditation practice that it requires no effort at all because focused awareness has become the default state of the mind.

CHAPTER THIRTY-THREE

The Five Hindrances

When we take up intensive meditation, we soon discover that our practice can give rise to a wide range of experiences—from very unpleasant to very pleasant, and innumerable degrees in between—but also that it regularly runs into certain obstructions and distractions. These can be anything from feeling incredibly sluggish to feeling agitated and unable to sit still; from wanting to lie down and take it easy to being unusually annoyed by people or the surroundings; and from analysing and questioning the meditation method, to experiencing an overwhelming amount of fantasising or obsessive planning for the future.

In the texts reputed to be the earliest teachings of the Buddha, he breaks down these challenging states into five categories, known as the Five Hindrances. It's fascinating and encouraging to consider that—whether the meditator was training way back in the Buddha's time or now, was a man or woman, old or young, educated or not, this clan group or that—we all face the same variety of challenges when training the mind. So these five categories have a long and distinguished track record of nailing the difficult experiences you're likely to face. Understanding them will help you know when they're present and even give you means to overcome them. And it's vital that you overcome them. The original term for hindrance, the Pali word *nīvaraṇa*, also means obstacle, and it helps to think of these five challenges as obstacles to your progress. Failing to overcome them means we'll be stuck at the starting blocks.

It is normal in the early stages of meditation practice to engage with these difficult experiences as if they are true representations of our mind or reality. For example, when the mind takes us down the path of stressing about something or wanting to change something in our proximity, it's usually not about that something and instead is just the mind doing its best to avoid still, calm observation of the here and now. So an important realisation in these early stages is to see these events for what they are and free ourselves from entanglement with them by consistently returning to the meditation, over and over. Eventually we will overcome them and ascend to new levels of experience in our practice.

As we dive into examining the hindrances, it's important to note they are labelled with imperfect translations of linguistic concepts from the ancient language of Pali. So it's worthwhile understanding the intent of the original word rather than taking the modern English word at face value.

The hindrances come in two pairs and a leftover. Let's look at them closely.

1) Desire and 2) Aversion

Kāmacchanda from the Pali language is typically rendered into English as sensual desire, but the original term covers a wide scope: everything from overwhelming lust, to a subtle interest in something mildly comfortable like relaxing on a sofa. So it includes such diverse experiences you may come upon on retreat as sexual fantasies, hunger for food and drink, a yearning to lie down and get comfortable, wanting to change your circumstances such as making the time go quicker or the room be quieter, enjoying wallowing in thoughts of past glories, and indulging in dreams of future plans. It covers anything where you experience a want of any kind, no matter how weak or strong.

Vyāpāda is the opposite and is usually translated as ill will or aversion. Any time there is hatred or anger arising in your mind, you're feeling aversion. This could manifest as disliking your posture, feeling ill will towards another meditator, considering fleeing from the retreat, or even hatred towards oneself or others.

But, someone may ask, these feelings are such common everyday experiences, why are they hindrances? Good question! Because they keep the mind leaning towards wanting or leaning towards hating. For the mind to become concentrated, it must settle into a centred and balanced state with no inclining towards this or inclining away from that. Desire and aversion are like winds that blow the sails of a boat back and forth, ensuring it never finds even keel and settles into stillness.

Ultimately, mental states are just to be known and observed, not reacted to. If you are aware a hindrance is happening, you are already a big step ahead of where you began. To be lost in thoughts about a happy past memory means the mind is unwittingly revelling in desire for those things it cannot have, and is far from doing the practice. To be lost in thoughts of revenge means the mind is blindly wallowing in anger towards someone, and again is in the wrong place for achieving growth in the practice. When we bring attention to the mind's activities and know these attitudes as unhelpful, the mind can let go and return to the object of meditation. It's as simple as that. But be warned, in the early stages of a retreat, it will take more than a few instances of pulling the attention back to overcome this. The poor habits of our daily lives take time to change. Patience is key!

3) Sloth and Torpor, 4) Restlessness and Worry

These two hindrances are actually made up of two parts each, but being closely related, each pair is presented together.

The first pair, *thīna-middha*, translated as the rather outmoded words Sloth and Torpor, refers to when the mind becomes sleepy, inactive, and unresponsive. Which might sound quite peaceful and relaxing, but once you've experienced it, you'll know it can be very unpleasant. Sloth and Torpor is especially common in the hour or two after a big meal. To me, it feels like the mind is drowning in molasses. No matter how you strive, you cannot bring effective attention to anything. You may also experience falling asleep during the sitting meditation. I once saw a snoozing meditator gradually slumping down until they were laid out on the floor snoring!

It's possible to react to this state of affairs with self-blame as if we're not working hard enough, but in fact this is a natural response of the mind to the discipline of attention training. Sometimes the mind is facing aspects of its reality it finds unpalatable or uninteresting, and one way out is for it to shut down. The good news is that Sloth and Torpor passes if you continue to sit patiently with it and keep paying attention the best you can. Eventually you'll notice the mind starts to re-arise, brighten, and become active and alert again.

It's important to note, while your instinct may be to give in and go lie down for a nap, that that will only prolong this hindrance in your practice. Also, in some meditation methods there are means for dealing with the generating of energy in the mind, such as quickly shifting attention around, breathing heavily a few times, and so on. Ask your teacher for advice when you run into this one.

The other pair is *uddhacca-kukkucca*, or Restlessness and Worry, which should be self-explanatory. It covers the gamut from feeling a frequent drive to shift, fidget, or get up and take a break, to feeling sad about past events and worried about future ones. Together they have the shared capacity to keep the mind from calming down, settling into a gentle routine, and maintaining stable attention. While we're here, let me point out that the training in morality, discussed under its own heading, can eventually cause a decrease in worry or remorse as one learns to avoid the kinds of actions that lead to a mind burdened by regrets and misgivings.

Overcoming this pair of obstacles involves settling the attention on one object of observation and keeping it there for as long as you can. The good news is, like the other hindrances, it is a temporary state of the practice and will eventually pass away of its own accord. Again, the important point is to stick with it and not give in. Remember, you're training the mind to overcome the ennui of its past habits and this is best supported by staying present through the challenges.

5) Sceptical Doubt

Vicikicchā means doubt or perplexity. While the hindrances can be a frustration, a bore, or even downright awful, I find this one the most interesting.

First of all, it stands alone and has no partner or opposite. Second, it can manifest as a kind of mind game. The other four hindrances are somewhat clear when they are present: feeling aroused or sleepy is easy to spot, and feeling angry or sorrowful about the past is clear too. But Sceptical Doubt can invade our thoughts by masquerading as an apparently reasonable and timely line of inquiry.

Sceptical Doubt refers to a pattern of reactivity the mind gets entangled in when it finds the practice difficult and wants a way out. It brings up challenges, often intellectual in nature, around such matters as whether the teacher knows what they're talking about, whether the method is really any good, whether this school is a cult, whether this training is doing me any good or my time would be better spent getting back to the chores and challenges of my daily life, and so on. And one of the most insidious manifestations of this hindrance is doubts about our own ability or suitability for the practice. If we don't see this hindrance for what it is and instead fall into engaging with it, it can lead us on a merry dance and even steer us down the path of quitting the retreat.

The obvious answer might be to simply make up your mind to accept the teacher, the teachings, the method, and the retreat as they are, as well as confidence in your own abilities, and get on with the training. But this is easier said than done. It certainly pays to have settled in your mind prior to the retreat that you have made a good choice, that you really want to learn these things, and that you're determined to see it through no matter what challenges arise. But all the same Sceptical Doubt can be difficult to spot and overcome because it comes clothed in our own most private and particular thoughts, concerns, and memories.

Sceptical Doubt also represents one instance in meditation where your cultural background can make a big difference. To have been raised in a setting where the Buddha, his teachings, his path to liberation, and the current crop of teachers who are passing it on are all beyond question, then this hindrance doesn't tend to hold you up much. Conversely, if you've developed a penchant for intellectual rumination, including questioning everything you see and hear in the new setting of a retreat, you're likely to find this a big challenge.

The good news—it's great there's always some in there—is that it can be overcome. This is done by diligently noticing these trips into analysis, speculation, questioning, and doubting, and then pulling the focus back to the object. Over and over and over. Eventually the mind gets bored of these unrewarded excursions because we tend not to waste effort on things that don't yield results. Or you'll begin to get enough of a taste of strong concentration and insight into the fruits of the practice that the mind will give up on scepticism and doubt, and then you'll find your practice moving ahead unhindered.

You may have noticed the lesson that shines through in each of these hindrances is to push on and work through them rather than wallow in or flee from them, as they are all just temporary states of mind that will pass. Facing them down will eventually send them scurrying and your practice will ascend to new levels.

CHAPTER THIRTY-FOUR

Maps

Sooner or later you will discover that among the texts of some traditions are detailed descriptions, known as maps, of the meditation terrain that a meditator will traverse. Some of this information may be guarded closely by teachers, while some of it may be available in the public domain. The maps are usually ancient textual descriptions of the sequential states of mind or experiential milestones that represent stages of a journey towards a culmination point or breakthrough. They are usually couched in complex and archaic terms that can be difficult for a modern meditator to decipher, potentially leaving the reader with a vague and poorly defined understanding. And it's important as you start out that you understand the purpose of and hazards in this information.

When young meditators reach out for advice on where to go to meditate, there is sometimes an overabundance of map terminology peppered throughout their emails or speech. They may have little retreat time behind them, but they apparently have a large amount of reading about and delving into the maps there in its stead. The teachings stipulate that too much of this kind of knowledge—known as excessive wisdom—leads to craftiness. That is, looking for ways to game the meditation project. This is not a criticism of anyone. It's completely natural: we are conditioned to seek results as efficiently as possible. Besides, I also did it back in the day. But that means I can confirm it isn't as helpful as we might hope.

The maps were typically set down in ancient times by scholar-monks who compiled the materials existing at the time to help meditators find their way. In recent times there has been a plethora of books and websites distilling this ancient content into modern interpretations, some faithful, some not. In my opinion, it is also the case that these teachings were usually intended for advanced meditators and teachers. The terminology and background knowledge required were too specialised for the uninitiated to benefit from in the absence of expert guidance. Furthermore, purists within some traditions consider these compilations apocryphal or antithetical, making them controversial and possibly unreliable. So, while these collections of advice and waypoints for the journey to an Enlightenment of one kind or another may represent valuable cultural and religious heritage, they can also cause confusion, craving, goal-seeking, and downright disorientation at the individual level, as well as sectarian conflicts on a broader scale.

I cannot say it strongly enough that, at the beginning stages of anyone's meditation journey, we do not need to know these texts in detail and they will not help our practice. To be curious is perfectly reasonable and we can all anticipate what happens when we are told not to open a certain book. But you only need to know that, should you persevere in the development of your practice and when the time comes, the maps may give you some helpful guidance, especially when gradually revealed to you by an experienced teacher.

To air the opposite view of some Westerners: the more informed you are the better, and familiarity with the maps is important for the progress of your meditation journey. Based on my experience as a devotee of maps from the very start of my practice and that of countless others I have spoken to, this knowledge is simply not helpful *in the early stages*. There comes a time when it can help but, ultimately, if someone cannot progress naturally without investigating what comes next and then entertaining expectations about it, they should instead spend time with a good teacher to work through that stage.

A useful line of enquiry to guide you through this matter is to ask why the meditation path of progress requires that you know all of this detail, rather than allowing the developments to unfold naturally. It suggests some kind of artifice is at work if a meditator needs to know what the upcoming stages look like in order for them to occur. You will find in the more traditional training environments, such as monasteries in Asia, teachers rarely discuss these matters with a student, and if they do, it's usually obliquely. They operate on the belief a meditator will develop the faculties to achieve progress without explicit prompting. Of course, this approach calls for a lot of patience and trust, which it is fair to say are less common among Western meditators.

Alternatively, if you have absorbed the descriptions of certain meditation experiences or attainments and then go on to practise the technique, you're likely to find the mind searching for those outcomes, even going so far as to strive to produce them based on expectations. Or you may find yourself working to connect up the potentially vast array of things arising in your practice with those complex and ambiguous descriptions in the texts. Let me stress it again: in no way will this help your practice progress and may instead hinder it.

Recall the point of wisdom mentioned before:

The attitude we bring to the practice is as important as the practice itself.

Many of the discoveries and changes that can occur on a meditation journey are by their nature subconscious and spontaneous, and as such they are arrived at by a kind of naïve exploration. Setting out to deliberately stumble on something you don't understand and weren't supposed to know was there just doesn't work. It's how people end up speciously joining dots and arriving at magnificent conclusions about their practice, and in turn about themselves, which may be far from true.

Furthermore, depending on one's psychological predisposition, a meditator may become so focused on the details of how the stages and milestones are reputed to occur that they fail to actually experience the events themselves. Or they may unwittingly engage in generating entirely fake experiences out of their expectations. It's known as confusing the map for the territory. If you spend enough time on social media and online forums, you will see plenty of people on these wild goose chases.

Here's a couple of fictional examples common to online discussion forums.

"For a few moments, I couldn't locate any sense of self. Does this mean I've achieved [X level]?" In fact, spontaneous moments of non-dual awareness—where the sense of a viewer or subject appears to be absent—are

common in meditation and even in daily life, such as when we "lose" ourselves in flow states. You'll also find that decisively pinning down such an experience as a sense of the viewer or subject is challenging, especially for a beginner, so it's easy to misinterpret that difficulty for evidence the sense of self has vanished and we are now a certifiable holy one.

"I was sitting there meditating when it seemed like my whole experience disappeared and then after a while I became aware again. I think I had a [X experience]." It takes some time for a meditator to progress beyond the stage where they sometimes slip into a stunned or sleepy reverie, barely conscious, and return to alertness with a sense of having been absent. Such moments of apparent ceasing of consciousness are usually no more than a symptom of a drifting or sleepy mind.

Let me be clear that such experiences can also be the real thing. But an online discussion with an assortment of strangers of unknown qualifications is no way to determine what's really going on in your practice and can instead be an invitation to fall into believing whatever is most pleasing. Spending time in the company of a reputable teacher presents by far the best chance for both making progress and finding out where you are on the journey.

There's so much craving for attainments that goes on in maps-driven meditation that our egos are powerfully drawn to overestimations of our achievements. So let's stop and take a hit of rationality. It has become a cliché among scientists to describe the human brain as the most complex structure in the known universe. Consider the fact that our central nervous system is built upon millions of sensory receptors throughout the body which feed countless signals per second into a brain consisting of billions of cells, which communicate to give rise to trillions of synapse connections. And yet we personally know of none of this neuronal activity, only the resulting impressions of consciousness via sensory experiences. Without our know-how or input, the brain creates staggering degrees of imagination, interpretation, abstraction, and pattern-making, emerging out of layers upon layers of self-generated meaning and self-identification. Also consider that, in the everyday experience of the untrained human being, most of this cognitive activity is dulled down or filtered out so we can focus on mundane functions. So, if we have that human sit down and bring carefully practised, microscopic attention to every rapid change throughout their body-mind field, they are sure to stumble upon heightened levels of perception never experienced before.

As you can imagine, these novel vistas can open us up to mind-blowing sensory and cognitive experiences, for which we could easily find justifications to invest them with grand meanings. There can be the speeding up of perceptions, blinding lights in the mind, cascading or pulsing sensations throughout the body, extreme identity perspective shifts, vivid imaginings that can leave us awestruck, a degree of stillness and silence so unusual we wonder if time has stopped or we have ceased to breathe. Such experiences don't happen frequently or for everyone, but events along these lines do arise for some people some of the time. And while they might be dazzling and lead to extravagant claims of oneness with the universe or leaving one's body or abandoning the sense of self, we need to be on our guard against investing these fleeting moments with more importance than they warrant.

A general rule is to wait a year after any kind of major event to see if it unfolds into, sustains, or brings about any real change. Considering the meditation journey can be punctuated with unusual moments which will pass as quickly as they arose, you'd be safe in betting any individual experience is just the bleeps and burps of our extraordinarily complex central nervous system touching on new heights and dimensions. Such dismissive scepticism is the best way to approach these events to ensure you don't become the next guru wannabe on social media claiming to have attained some kind of supreme status. If, with further training and hindsight, it turns out that your indifference was wrongly applied, then congratulations! What's more, you and everyone around you will be better off for your cautious modesty.

Please note that major and important attainments are certainly possible through intensive meditation practice. For many people it's the entire point of the practice. But for most of us these attainments take a lot of patient and steady work. It is unhelpful in the extreme to compare our progress to others', including taking as gospel truth the many stories we encounter online about people achieving significant breakthroughs in remarkably short periods of practice. Maybe it really happened, but maybe it didn't. That's no slight on them: they could simply be mistaken, or perhaps it's true because they have extraordinary capabilities the rest of us don't have. Countless times I've been utterly convinced of certain developments in my practice, only to round another corner and discover I was completely wrong. I have learned to laugh at myself often on this journey. You have to get used to being wrong a lot when searching for what is deeply hidden and difficult to find, especially when you have been primed to want to find something as soon as possible so as to keep up with everyone else.

Each of us brings our own unique mix of psychological history and reactivity as well as intellectual and spiritual motivations to the task of meditation, so progress is never uniform or predictable across any cross section of meditators. If a breakthrough is real, you'll know it to your own satisfaction sooner or later. Along the way, obsessively studying and following the maps is likely to lead you down many a sidetrack. I for one have become very familiar with the sidetracks over the years so I can firmly recommend the humbler approach. Best just to take a step at a time and see what the journey reveals to you.

CHAPTER THIRTY-FIVE

Faith

What does faith have to do with meditation? For modern Westerners, particularly of a secular or atheist bent like myself, we have developed a deep suspicion of all things faith-based. While you may be aware that Buddhism is lived as a religion in many countries, you may also think of Buddhism as lacking the monotheistic elements of the Abrahamic religions and therefore being more of a rational philosophy. And certainly the popular modern literature on Buddhism often presents it in association with concepts like science, psychology, and philosophy. So it can be surprising or even discouraging for some of us that, in Buddhist meditation training, faith turns up frequently. But as is often the case, ancient words translated into English don't always have a perfect modern counterpart. Let's take a closer look.

First, the Pali term *saddhā* (Sanskrit: *śraddhā*), typically translated as faith, can also be equally well rendered as confidence or trust. And what the term is really getting at is not belief in unfounded claims about gods and creation myths. Instead, it's about trusting in the original teacher, his teachings, and the monastic community that lives to propagate the teachings, so we can get on with focusing on the training itself. If we fail to do this, we may end up a slave to our natural inclination to engage in endless internal debates about the teachings, concepts, and practices we encounter in meditation training.

As stated in the section on the Five Hindrances, the mind's tendency towards hindrance number five, Sceptical Doubt, can have a crippling effect on our meditation. If you think of scepticism and doubting as a defence mechanism arising out of our natural conceit to believe we already know what's what, then you'll understand we should do away with it as quickly as we can when we sit down to meditate. And this is why faith—or confidence, if you prefer—is central to good meditation. A calm, peaceful mind free of the turbulence of doubt-fuelled thinking is key to meditation progress.

In a traditional Buddhist training environment, you're likely to encounter people who have been raised as Buddhists with a deep reverence and respect for the original teacher and his teachings. They tend not to spend any mental energy on questioning or doubting, and the rumours are that such people have a big head-start over those of us who prefer to exercise our conceit muscles on every new concept we run across.

It also helps to study a little about who the Buddha was and what he discovered about the human condition, so as to fire up the desire to commit to the training and learn more. For suggestions, see Further Resources.

When we come into contact with a new paradigm, our cognitive immune system is likely to leap into action and reject it outright. But if we really want to engage with it in a sincere test of its verifiability, it pays to bring the new idea in, try it on for size, and give it a chance to be proven or falsified.

No one is suggesting we should blindly accept anything. Before you begin the training, it's a good idea to investigate the teachings you'll encounter on retreat. You should read and delve to satisfy your curiosity. This will reduce the burden of practice-related analysis in the midst of training. It also helps to notice when the mind gets edgy and starts finding intellectual investigation of the teacher and the method excessively attractive and intriguing. Noticing this helps us remove our attention from the analysis and bring it back to the object of meditation. I have known of people becoming embroiled in this kind of analysis paralysis, who then quit a retreat because they fell for the doubts that arose in their overactive minds.

Another major way that an absence of faith can undermine our training is the lack of confidence in our own abilities. It is not unusual for us to have developed throughout our lives an unhelpful mental habit of criticising or attacking ourselves when we don't get the results we expected. A common experience in meditation training is to run up against agitation, frustration, boredom, disappointment, and the like, and then to resort to our usual response of finding fault in ourselves, sometimes fuelled by looking around the meditation hall and feeling sure that no one else is going through what we are struggling with.

The truth is *everyone* runs up against obstacles in their practice. *Everyone* needs to overcome challenges in order to progress. *Everyone* sometimes feels driven to quit. These are natural occurrences during the training, but they're also not to be worried over because eventually we move beyond them. I noticed after a couple of retreats that self-acceptance began to arise and replace the old habit of self-blame. It was such a pleasant change to notice the fading away of the old harsh judging voice and the arising in its place of a new calm voice of "Oh well, keep going, it'll go better next time."

For encouragement, remind yourself that no one picks up a guitar for the first time and plays beautifully. No one picks up a camera and right away makes extraordinary pictures. And no one starts learning a language and can instantly chatter away. In the same way, training the mind to overcome its old, unhelpful habits takes time and patience. We can all do it. The only difference between those who excel and those who don't is how long they stick with it.

And finally, faith—or confidence—arises naturally as a result of our meditation gaining momentum. When we have clear-cut experiences or insights, the mind automatically gets a boost of confidence that leads to energy and onwards to practice growth and development. This is a good example of how meditation yields its secrets to those who stick it out and keep going until the fruits begin to manifest.

Having confidence in yourself and seeing worth in the time you're investing in the practice both help you put aside doubts and push on. This is how faith works in meditation practice. No supernatural beliefs needed!

CHAPTER THIRTY-SIX

Mindfulness vs. Concentration

A variety of mental skills and capabilities are developed during meditation practice. The two you should understand best are mindfulness and concentration.

In short, mindfulness is about staying aware and present in each consecutive moment during a session. Concentration is about keeping the attention on one point. They both involve maintaining consistent attention over time. It's just the way we do this that differs. See also the related section on the two main strands of Buddhist meditation, Samatha (tranquility, involving concentration) and Vipassana (insight, involving mindfulness).

The main difference between the two is that mindfulness involves keeping the mind open to observe whatever is occurring, including shifting our awareness to each newly arising experience. Whereas concentration is developed by keeping the attention on a single point to the exclusion of other occurrences.

Let's look at some examples. If you're practising mindfulness, as is the case in a Vipassana context, you might be observing sensations of the breath at the abdomen as it rises and falls with each breath, but then the mind suddenly switches to the awareness of a thought, observes it, then switches again to the awareness of a sound nearby, observes it, and then returns to the abdominal sensations of the rise and fall of the breath. This means the attention is moving around, sometimes rapidly and quite a lot. That's not to say mindfulness consists of the mind racing around randomly. Typically, when a sitting session has become calm and settled, the attention tends to stay on only a few main sources of sensory activity within the body-mind field.

In concentration practice, you might be observing the breath sensations as they appear on the upper lip, just below the nostrils, which is a common practice known as *Ānāpāna*. You manage to keep the attention stable on the sensations there through each in-breath and out-breath, over and over, for a period of, say, ten seconds, after which the mind is captured by a thought and wanders away. At some point, maybe after a few seconds, you notice the mind is thinking so you bring the focus of the attention back to the upper lip, catch onto the sensations of the breath there, and continue watching the breath come in and go out. As you do this, you may notice thoughts are frequently tugging at the attention to pull it away. Without engaging in thoughts about this, you just keep turning the attention to the breath sensations. With enough practice, the attention will happily stay on those sensations for longer and longer periods. In the early stages, don't be disappointed if your concentration only remains stable for a few seconds at a time. You are training to overcome a lifetime of mind-wandering and mind-hopping from thought to thought, so it will take time, patience, and effort.

Now, if you were paying close attention to the above, you may have noticed some overlaps. In concentration practice, when the mind wanders off to daydreams and thoughts, it's mindfulness that catches this, allowing us to pull the attention back to the upper lip. And while in mindfulness practice, provided there are no persistent distractions, your attention on, say, the sensations of the rise and fall of the abdomen will become increasingly concentrated until it is staying nicely on a detailed aspect of those sensations for an extended period. Which is basically concentration.

So it's fair to say they are not mutually exclusive but in fact overlap and even support each other. It's also true they are different routes to approaching meditation practice. It's enough in the early stages of your training to know whether you should be focused on mindfulness or concentration as the first order of business. Later on, be careful of becoming indoctrinated by a tradition into siding with their particular method. This is a common feature of the meditation world and brings no benefit to the individual.

CHAPTER THIRTY-SEVEN

Conceit

> *conceit (noun)*
> *favourable opinion, especially: excessive appreciation of one's worth or virtue.*
> Source: www.merriam-webster.com/dictionary

Insofar as Buddhist meditation is a project of seeing through our egocentrism, then bringing a big dose of conceit to a retreat is likely to undermine the entire enterprise. Conceit and its effect on our meditation are vital to understand because we all have some measure of conceit in our personalities. The term covers the gamut from somewhat harmless self-love, to the self-absorption of egotism, to the sociopathy of narcissism.

Conceit—or excessive self-regard—is as central to the human psyche as our spine is to our anatomy. And it makes sense that we humans are endowed with a generous helping of excessive self-appreciation. An organism driven by confidence as well as a persistent and energetic focus on its own concerns is more likely to overcome obstacles to survival. And here we are, the human species, thriving on planet Earth, at least in population terms. But following this instinct for self-concern in our modern daily lives can also undermine our broader happiness by bringing us into conflict with others. When we view the world through a lens of conceit, we have trouble granting others respect and their due rights, as well as being able to see our own true worth in the self-sacrificing service of others. When everyone is giving rein to conceit, we end up with a world awash in self-centredness, personality clashes, entrenched views, and conflict everywhere from the checkout counter to our social media feeds.

For the record, I am not pointing fingers or seeking to ridicule anyone. I warn of these flaws precisely because I am subject to them too. And probably still often am. Conceit is common to us all to one degree or another, so it's helpful to learn to spot it.

Let's take a moment to recall an example of ugly human behaviour.

Got one? Now try the same with an example of beautiful behaviour.

Let's compare them. What do you find?

I expect you'll discover the difference has a lot to do with the degree or absence of conceit on display. It's fair to say all of us would like to move along that spectrum from ugly to beautiful.

People raised in a traditional Asian Buddhist setting tend to approach the practice of meditation with deep reverence and respect. This generally results in a crop of local meditators whose personal concerns align with a wholehearted and gracious commitment to the training.

Western folks, on the other hand, come from a culture with little contemporary interest in its own ancient teachings, let alone those of distant cultures. We can see the obsession with newness all around us in daily life. This year's iPhone is instantly superior to last year's, despite there being little actual difference. A 2023 book immediately supersedes any earlier publication, despite being largely based on the earlier. And today's angle on historical events makes all past ones obsolete. So consider how much harder it is to grasp that, thousands of years ago in a faraway land, people had already developed some advanced insights that today we can still learn an enormous amount from.

When we enter a different cultural environment and encounter these unusual ideas stemming from such ancient roots, we indulge in a lot of questioning and doubting. As covered in the section on the Five Hindrances, one of the main obstacles to effective practice is Sceptical Doubt. And when you examine this hindrance closely, you'll see that confronting a new idea with disrespectful tyre-kicking is an exercise in conceit that many of us automatically act out. We tend not to accept ideas new to our cultural or ideological paradigm without running them through a self-serving wringer of confirmation bias in the hope of reasserting the correctness and sanctity of our own worldview. It hardly needs stating this is unhelpful in meditation training.

Or there's the conceit of wanting to dodge submission to rules, to ensure I am in charge of my time and body and activities. In my case, for example, I often started out with an unacknowledged conceit about the circumstances of the retreat. Sure, I had to do certain things their way, but I also brought items like coffee or snacks so I could indulge in some luxuries along the way, unconsciously acting out the exercising of my self-centred will, even to the detriment of my practice. After a few days, I would spot what game was really being played and put the temptations away.

Whatever our situation, it is best to approach the retreat intending to let go of expectations, to commit wholeheartedly to the training regimen, to accept graciously whatever we're given no matter how simple, and to remind ourselves of my favourite adage:

> *Our comfort zone is the place where nothing interesting ever happens.*

This could be done as a heartfelt resolution spoken to ourselves each day prior to the retreat. For example, "I commit to letting go of expectations, and to give every effort to learning the practice." Give it a try. You will be surprised how much our subconscious can be swayed by these self-focused directives.

While on retreat, we should notice when our minds rebel against having to bend to changes or accept the unexpected. Such moments contain valuable lessons if we stay present to them and face up to what they show us about ourselves. When others are bowing upon arrival at the meditation hall, give it a try and see how it grates on us to bend down and submit to a higher ideal than our own needs in every moment. Bring attention to the details of the meditation instructions and make a personal commitment to observe and practise every part of it rather than compare and question and speculate. Bring awareness to the judging thoughts that arise in our minds about the other retreatants and replace them with kind and respectful thoughts. To quote a teacher's wise words to me during a time of aggravation:

> *People often come to meditation out of suffering, so let go of judging and instead consider the burden they may be carrying.*

To sum up, two common reasons people cite for going on a retreat are to get to know themselves better and to become a better person. Apart from the obviously conceited nature of these goals, they can also be noble intentions, arising out of the awareness that we are often the source of our own and others' unhappiness. But to approach either of these goals with sincerity requires a readiness to face our true nature with frank and unwavering honesty. When we bring clear self-awareness to moments of conceit, it tends to vanish like a vampire in the daylight. And in its absence we can open to the possibility of personal growth free of delusions about our self-importance.

CHAPTER THIRTY-EIGHT

Enlightenment

No topic in the field of meditation is anywhere near as interesting or controversial as that of Enlightenment: what it is, if it's possible, whether enlightened people exist today, what they're like, what meditation method will get you there, and so on. There are lots of books on it. Many hours of online videos and podcasts about it. Internet forums where people debate its many facets. Teachers and meditators who claim to have achieved it. And sceptics who say it cannot be done. To further complicate matters, there are differing models and systems from one tradition's sub-sect to the next, let alone the larger doctrinal and cultural differences from, say, Sri Lanka to Japan.

This topic is a minefield, what with all the sectarian debates and emotional reactivity that it inspires, not to mention the complexity. But it's undeniably important for Western meditators: Enlightenment is discussed widely in one form or another, including by prominent teachers, and meditators are increasingly willing to admit it's the reason they took up intensive meditation.

I have elected to use the word Enlightenment with a capital E throughout this book to highlight that the word choice is not to be taken lightly and should be called out. The translation was adopted by nineteenth-century European scholars from the Pali term *bodhi*, meaning awakening, from which the term Buddha (awakened one) is derived. My view is that Enlightenment is an unfortunate choice that gives Westerners cause to think of some kind of unrealistic mystical status akin to a god. By capitalising it and ironically placing it front and centre in this discussion, I hope to call it out a little. Feel free to substitute it as you read for something more helpful like awakening. All such terms are gesturing towards something difficult to see. The challenge is to approach an understanding of what that is, then you can apply whichever word you like.

Let's start with the basics. Is there such a thing as Enlightenment? If the word calls to mind a holy Buddha-like being floating in a lotus posture while emanating beams of golden light in all directions, you could be excused for thinking it's a bunch of religious mysticism. Conversely, if someone conflates it with the European Enlightenment, the period of rapid scientific and intellectual development in the seventeenth and eighteenth centuries, they might think it suggests having mysteriously attained a supreme omniscience, able to see and know everything by sitting on a cushion. Again, you could be forgiven for seeing the concept as mystical nonsense.

We may become even more sceptical when we research online and encounter people claiming this supposedly grand and high achievement from some casual practice on their sofa, or from one brief retreat, or from having met a teacher they claim is the only one capable of bestowing it, or other such incredible and unverifiable claims. You might also encounter offerings of Enlightenment, awakening, and other ill-defined concepts in the ubiquitous yoga studios around Western cities that sell access to fashionable spirituality for high monthly fees. The vague and dubious application of such terms in modern spiritual scenes is disheartening and it is reasonable to react with disdain to the whole project.

But consider for a moment there is a series of important cognitive changes that intensive meditation leads us through. And the common conception of these achievements is distorted by many centuries of traditional religious narrative-making. If those religious narratives overstate what it is and understate how accessible it is to anyone willing to do the work, it makes sense that modern people would be perplexed and sceptical. Add to that the Buddha's injunction against monks and nuns talking openly of their meditation attainments (lest they be mistaken and thereby mislead people) and you can see that Enlightenment has become the secretive stuff of legends.

And yet this is despite the earliest known texts showing the Buddha routinely exhorting everyone to strive for liberation "in this very life". He was not known to suggest only certain people under special circumstances could attain it. To demonstrate that Enlightenment is available to everyone regardless of their specifics, the texts relate the tale of Angulimala the mass murderer who, upon encountering the wisdom of the Buddha's teachings, had a change of heart and renounced violence to become a monk, and eventually attained the highest release. Remember that the fifth of the Five Hindrances is Sceptical Doubt, which most certainly has a powerful hold over the mind, so we owe it to ourselves to be on our guard.

* * *

The key to understanding Buddhist Enlightenment is to see it as the cure for an illness. In the Buddha's assessment, we are all mentally unwell by default. The very structure of our consciousness ensures we experience our existence in a deluded way that leads to profound and all-pervasive suffering. By purifying the mind through training to the extent that it sees through and abandons the illness, we can become well. As you can see, those are some big claims, so naturally you should delve into the teachings for further details on consciousness, its unwholesome nature, and the abandonment of such.

In the same way that getting over a cold is simply the departure of something we didn't want, Enlightenment refers to the letting go of cognitive flaws, rather than the gaining of something like supreme knowledge. One does not "gain" Enlightenment per se, rather one sees through that which blocks pure perception. Perhaps you already see the unsuitability of the E word, when what we are talking about would be better described as Letting-Go or Release or Seeing-Through. Admittedly, they're not as catchy and would not get past the marketing department.

There is a variety of models and ways of describing the illness and the cure, but let's use one called the Ten-Fetter Model. The fetters, like mental handcuffs, are aspects of cognition bestowed upon us by our biology and neuropsychology (or fate or *kamma* or however your worldview likes to see it), which are delusional and harmful. According to this model, via meditation the mind sees through and "loses" the fetters at certain stages along the journey. That is, Enlightenment unfolds through numerous stages, so one can be partially or fully enlightened, depending on how many fetters have been abandoned.

Let's take a look at the first and, in my opinion, the most influential of the fetters. Known as Identity View, it refers to the way our mind, by default, sets up an identification of its conceptual sense of self through experiences that come in via the senses and arise in the mind. For example, when light enters the eyes, at a subconscious level the mind experiences it as "I see light," and when an experience of sensory pleasure is there, the mind notes it as "I enjoy pleasure," and when a thought arises in the mind, there is an understanding "I think a thought." It also operates on the level of claiming ownership of everything within its scope. This is "my body" and "my thought". And we end up dwelling in a world where everything exists only in relation to me, my view of it, and its value to me. That tree is my tree that I see with my eyes and which is shading my house and therefore pleases me. Those people that I hear saying things I don't like and who contradict my views are annoying and unsettling to me and therefore I want them gone.

When extrapolated to include our entire range of daily experiences, we become invested and embroiled on a self-centred level in every moment of experience as well as every thought that arises. We become tightly entangled with the belief there is a unique and permanent soul or personality here that by its nature must persist beyond the current moment. Imagine how frightening is the inevitable prospect of growing old and suffering illness when we are invested in the idea that our reason for living is the acting out of our free will and the achieving of our ideal of happiness. Imagine how nightmarish the matter of death is to a mind that has become convinced it exists as a unique and permanent entity independent of the passing of time. And on a mundane level, imagine the angst of a mind whose illusion of self suffers criticisms, failures, attacks, or setbacks in society.

As meditative observation eventually shows us, in truth there is no experiencer or thinker, only the experience or the thought. So the enlightened "unfettered" perspective would be: "There is seeing" or "There is the seen," and "There is thinking" or "There is a thought." As a result, these experiences would no longer give rise to a cognitive performance of becoming invested in a self.

To be self-identified with everything that arises in one's body and mind is to become deeply invested in whether those things are good or bad, and whether one can control the outcomes to be more good than bad. The fact this entire relationship is built on incorrect assumptions means no matter how hard I crave it, I will not succeed in getting the outcomes I have invested my "self" in. Hence, to summarise part of the foundational Buddhist teaching of the Four Noble Truths: suffering is at the core, and craving is its cause.

It may strike you that little or none of this is apparent to the untrained mind so newcomers would not be quickly convinced. We may intuit something is amiss with our perception of our place in the scheme of things and that life just never sits quite right, but the critique the Buddha offered is hard to see. Legend tells us that, upon reflection after his Enlightenment, he decided that teaching these discoveries to people would be so hard, he should just retire and forget about it. Fortunately, a guest visited who persuaded him to strive to teach because "there are beings with little dust in their eyes". That is, some people will be able to understand, so it is worth going forth to teach. And sure enough, as we make progress along the journey, we gain increasing depths of insight into and familiarity with his discoveries, gradually removing the dust from our eyes.

The illusion of the sense of self described above is without doubt one of the more elusive features of the Buddhist teachings to gain a personal grasp of. But we should look closely at what an illusion is. No one is claiming "you" don't exist, only that the perception and understanding that make up the impression of a self in the centre of experience right here right now is flawed and mistaken.

Here's a clumsy analogy I cooked up earlier.

Imagine you are looking at a rainbow and you naturally accept it really is what it appears to be: a solid arch of colourful, somewhat transparent matter, permanent and unchanging as long as you watch it. Imagine also that you become deeply attached to the sensory perception of the rainbow, revelling in joy when it appears and suffering miserably when it is obscured from your view. You have become entangled and invested in the dualistic experience of "me" and "my rainbow".

Now a teacher takes you closer to the rainbow and shows you it is not a thing but a mere apparition arising out of light rays passing through water droplets. You discover it is only visible to one who stands at a certain place in a certain relationship to the light rays, all of it just a chance apparition of ever-changing elements that aren't yours and that you don't control. Suddenly you see it has no solid, dependable, substantial existence and in an instant your entire understanding of the rainbow changes. You have awakened to the true nature of the rainbow—it is just a concept—and your relationship to it has changed forever.

After this breakthrough, there is still a sensory experience unfolding inside your mind that you outwardly consent to go on calling a rainbow, but you no longer take it to be a solid and permanent reality existing outside your conceptual experience of it. As a result of this illusion-busting, a very important cognitive development has taken place: your fear of its going and your craving for its coming have gone. You are now in a new relationship to the rainbow experience and no longer have to endure the painful, turbulent pushing and pulling of the emotions around your previous illusory relationship to it. You calmly notice this deeper reality with clarity and wisdom, neither attached nor averse.

If we now recognise that the rainbow is a metaphor for the experience of our sense of self, our desire for its solid persistence in the world, and our terror at its disappearing or diminishing, we can see how profound the shift to seeing through it can be. If you don't like to label this important perceptual shift with a term so loaded and esoteric as Enlightenment, then by all means call it awakening, or myth-busting, or realisation.

If you enjoy seeing through illusions, see Further Resources for books that explore this topic and the implications for our grasp of reality.

Whatever label you choose, by now it should be clear there is a cognitive perspective shift. One doesn't receive new knowledge or ascend to anything higher. One simply experiences existence in a new and better way. But such illusory perceptions of ourselves and our identities, albeit only conceptual abstractions in our minds, have important real-world impacts in our lives. What may seem like small invisible details can in fact determine how we feel and behave, which determine how we affect other people, which in turn affects the outcomes of our many activities in the world.

The next part is my opinion and is a subject of much debate. The outcomes of people's attainments are not guaranteed, as people who have accomplished high goals within their meditation practice are still capable of failing to live a thoroughly transformed existence. There's no doubt these meditation breakthroughs lead to changes in a person's perceptions and experience, but the outward displays of these changes are uncertain. In each person's psychological make-up there are too many variables for everyone to manifest the same developments in the same way. There are also some variables along the pathways to these breakthroughs, so each training journey can equip a person differently for how they will progress afterwards. Let's try the following metaphor. Passing these points in one's meditation development is like uncovering new tools in our toolkit. Tools can be used well, or poorly, or not at all. Two people could have the same tools: one produces refined woodwork while the other produces nothing of note. Judgements about the latent cognitive capabilities of those two individuals from their woodwork results would be baseless speculation.

Next, it's important to note that the shift happens only within the experience of the individual, so the change can only really be known by the person who has achieved it (possibly also a teacher who has closely examined their progress, but note the teacher's assessment is very unlikely to be on the public record). Some people achieve a practice breakthrough and do not realise it for a lengthy period, so consider how much less knowable it is to an external observer.

We've now arrived at one of the most important points in this topic: a person's claims to attainments can never be completely and independently verified. So while there is plenty of cause to accept these attainments are accessible in the real world, it's possible an individual may be mistaken (or may be misleading us) and for external observers to have no clue what to believe. To summarise, if someone makes a claim about their meditation attainments, you have absolutely nothing to help you decide whether to believe them but your gut feeling about their trustworthiness.

So what can you do? Would you believe someone claiming an attainment because they seem nice or seem to know what they're talking about? Alternatively, would you attribute to a person, such as a teacher, an attainment because they seem to exhibit certain characteristics you judge as enlightened? In the end, there is only one way to truly settle the matter: do it for yourself and see what you find.

And frankly, since Buddhist Enlightenment is fundamentally a solitary quest for individual salvation, the outcomes only affect and should only matter to the one who has "sweltered at the task". If a person is overly concerned with what others have achieved or what people believe about their practice outcomes, they probably need to knuckle down and keep working at it.

It's useful to consider our motivations for what we choose to believe about attainments. In every area of our lives, we are seeking to escape the unsatisfactoriness of our existence. Look around and you can see people working on this project of the self through hoarding material wealth, fame, or regard; pursuing self-improvement schemes; collecting accomplishments; or losing themselves in indulgences. When we bring this attitude to our meditation practice, it's logical we will seek high status goals or labels in the hope of finding an escape from our unsatisfactory lives. And this is as doomed to disappoint us as the other above-mentioned life projects.

* * *

Now let's take a look at what the Buddha is reputed to have discovered and achieved on his meditation journey. Gautama—the regular name by which he was known—spent some years training in well-established concentration techniques to observe sensations and mental states in incredibly fine detail. It's fair to say they trained hard in those days and they were hindered by less of the lifestyle distractions we have today. So his progress was fast.

Gautama eventually gained the insight that the mind is the generator of our perception of reality, including the apparition of permanent selfhood at the centre of our existence, which it achieves through an interpretation of sensory and mental experiences arising rapidly of their own accord in every moment. From this realisation sprang understandings about the nature of existence, consciousness, self-identification, and what causes suffering as a fundamental feature of our existence.

But there was another consequence of these deep and persistent investigations which separates him from mere philosophers who speak of ideas: he experienced a seeing through of these constructions, habits, beliefs, and views. By seeing through them, the illusions were gone, giving rise to a new psychological perspective free of the misapprehensions that had governed his experience of selfhood up to that point.

If we've covered all of that to some satisfaction, let me introduce a relatively new, modern faction comprised of both traditional Asian and secular Western players who have found a common ground on this topic. In the West, some people use the term Pragmatic Dharma to describe their rational and evidence-based approach, while in Asia you'll find emerging from Myanmar the matching conviction that meditation done properly leads to the outcomes described in ancient technical texts, with little or no religious observances required. It sounds kind of obvious—that to follow instructions should lead to the relevant results—but in religious circles this is dangerous thinking. In some traditionalists' eyes, to suggest one only has to walk the same path the founder walked and one can arrive at the same destination as him would be, ironically, tantamount to blasphemy. Anyway, their overlapping approach says the greatest heights of the Buddhist meditation path are available to anyone and everyone, because all it requires is an investment of time and effort. No saintly qualifications or third eyes required! They refer to ancient texts as well as modern meditation methods to define the levels of Enlightenment, the path ascending through them, and the unwholesome illusions that each stage is said to liberate one's mind from. This school of thought tends to run on a no-nonsense ethos of "do the work, get the results".

* * *

Sceptics have suggested that Enlightenment is mere religious or mystical brainwashing that meditators are trained to believe in. But this attitude reveals its own acknowledgement that the mind is capable of buying into false experiences and that people can fall so deeply into these falsehoods as to confuse them with reality. This we can all agree on. The cognitive activities you energetically immerse yourself in for hours every day will shape your mind and therefore configure your perceptions and resultant actions in the world. If you spend your days roiling in a quagmire of social media outrage, it will deeply shape you and it won't take long to see the effects on your life. How much more so will you become mired in narrowly constructed perceptions than if you commit all your mental energy to the constrained version of reality your biological hardwiring presents to your attention? The sceptics should ask themselves if they too are invested in illusions in their everyday lives. If they concede this could be the case and are interested to see into the nature of those illusions, they won't find a better method of investigation than meditation.

On the other hand, if training ourselves into the delusion that we are enlightened delivers those benefits, let's get together and delude ourselves into eliminating suffering from our lives! In all seriousness, since brainwashing is by definition reality-denying, it cannot deliver real, lasting change. And since wise and perceptive people would come to realise this, the practice would die out or shrink to a fringe curiosity. Instead, the opposite has been happening for thousands of years. Maybe there is something in this Buddhist meditation thing that is worth our time and effort after all. I keep repeating the message: there's only one way to find out.

The goal of Buddhist practice is not merely to train you into belief in a different paradigm but to free you from the above-mentioned delusions by bringing you into the awareness of how the mind actually works. When the practice is done right, you are simply observing what is there. If you just keep observing until the mind realises it is better off without the illusions, it lets them go. In a nutshell, that's the whole of the project. If you try doing anything else, such as creating mental images or states, or striving to experience certain kinds of highs, you will waste a lot of time, and hopefully a good teacher will be able to set you straight.

Finally, after spending some time in intensive training, the above doubts will vanish because you will see that it is in daily life we participate at both the individual and communal levels in addictive and unwholesome falsehoods, and it's only through meditative awareness that we become clear about the difference.

Just be on your guard about the mind's natural inclination towards the comforting myopia known as confirmation bias (putting emphasis on information that supports our beliefs while ignoring information that contradicts them), as well as projecting onto the practice our doubts and disinclination to do the hard work. It is a common pitfall to chop and change different methods when each one doesn't deliver our expected results in our desired time frame. But when we focus on achieving a clear and honest understanding no matter the outcome, rather than defensive adherence to an attractive or popular dogma, we are more likely to find our way to the right destination.

CHAPTER THIRTY-NINE

Dark Night

Some people swear it happens. Others swear it's made up. Whatever you believe, a dark stage seems to happen to plenty of us on the journey and, if you push on, it may happen to you. So while this topic comes across like an unpleasant public service announcement, I'd be remiss not to warn newcomers about what may lay ahead.

First, it's important to dispel a notion that meditation is a simple and straightforward path to happiness, with no potential drawbacks or shadow sides. There's a popular culture narrative that says meditation has only good outcomes, like eating fresh fruit and vegetables. In fact, it's not that simple.

In recent decades, the term Dark Night has come into common usage, especially online, as more people talk openly about difficulties they've experienced after retreat training. The term has been borrowed from the old Roman Catholic notion of a dark night of the soul: a period of crisis on the spiritual path. The current meditation usage refers specifically to changes that begin after the first significant insight breakthrough and can persist on and off for years afterwards. Meditators may complain of a range of problems revolving around a newly felt discontent with life. This can manifest as a loss of interest in careers, relationships, hobbies, exercise, eating, and so on. People talk of depression-related symptoms and emotional disturbance, culminating in difficulties continuing with a way of life that seemed clearer and more appealing prior to the retreat. Some people also report that their meditation becomes more difficult in terms of stress, discomfort, or mental anguish. They may quit meditation or else dive in with greater commitment. And finally, a common symptom is a new fascination (often obsessive) for topics around liberation like Enlightenment.

Described like this, the Dark Night may sound awful, but let's get some perspective to understand what it really tells us about the journey of mind-training. It's helpful to regard the Dark Night as a stage in one's meditation development, and so it *will* pass. It may take years, or it may be fairly quick. But it *will* pass.

Buddhist meditation is not about, as the mindfulness advertisements promise, becoming so chilled or self-aware that you get along better with everyone and become more successful. Nor should you expect to unlock hidden potential and "upgrade" yourself to become, again, more successful. Or whatever other conventional goals are sold to us through apps or self-help books, or by charlatan teachers. Some people go to meditation seeking unrealistic solutions to a variety of modern life woes without understanding that Buddhist meditation is actually very effective at certain things, but those things may not align with their expectations.

When we spend our lives deeply mired in distraction, mind-wandering, and ruminations about the past and the future, all centred on maintaining the illusion of a stable and unchanging experience of a self, we are missing out on a deeper and more powerful connection with actual experience. This insight is available through bringing very close attention to each moment as it's happening. The most reliable way we currently have to do this is meditation. It's really as simple as that. But it may not be obvious what that intensive experience of moment-to-moment reality can do to our minds.

There's a reason why we have become so habituated to constant distraction on the one hand and wallowing in sense pleasures on the other, both taking us away from being alert to the moment. It's obvious we're expending a lot of effort to avoid looking at some aspect of our cognition. So what's the problem?

The problem is what the Buddha called *dukkha* (rhymes with cooker), a Pali term (Sanskrit: *duḥkha*) variously translated into English as suffering, unsatisfactoriness, stress, misery, or pain. When we see the rapidly changing nature of our sensate reality, we are repulsed by the uncontrollable speed with which moments of experience arise and vanish, which also mirrors to our investigating minds that we too arise and vanish rapidly with no control over these fleeting moments of consciousness. This is a painful and fearful discovery, like looking down to find we are wobbling precariously on a tightrope over a bottomless chasm. In daily life, to avoid seeing this existential conundrum, which is actually apparent in every moment of consciousness if we just know where to direct our attention, we rush to find comfort in sense pleasures while simultaneously seeking to avoid the suffering and pain that reality can deal out to us. All of this is ultimately doomed to bring us back around to further dissatisfaction and suffering. This tragicomic neuropsychological pantomime pretty much sums up our entire life project.

We can observe this principle at work in the human world around us. Why do people devote so much of their lives to seeking material comforts, reliving sensual pleasures *ad nauseam*, and indulging as much as possible in entertainments and distractions? Why do people experience so much agitation, frustration, unhappiness, even hatred, if they don't get those comforts and pleasures when and how they wish? The answer is the same to all of these. They have a subconscious drive to distract themselves from the *dukkha* of the moment-to-moment awareness of ever-changing, ever-shifting, out-of-control, uncooperative reality. (If any of this explanation isn't quite working for you, be sure to come back to reread it after some retreat time.)

When we've devoted a lot of time and effort to bringing the mind into the present moment and holding it there consistently and sufficiently long enough that it gets the point, our worldview is going to shift. We may see that much of our life is spent mentally running from the truth of our experience and that our subconsciously driven efforts to achieve relief have led to no real, lasting improvement. We have become aware at a deep level that our experience of life is not what we'd taken it for. This may sound familiar to people who've been through a big life upset, especially the death of a loved one or nearly dying themselves, because these powerful reminders of the flimsy and whimsical nature of our existence hit us in a similar place. In Western culture we would mostly brush it off as a mental health episode or as a temporary adjustment like grieving, which implies that the old reality will eventually and comfortably reassert itself so we can continue on as if nothing happened.

In traditional meditation on the other hand, arriving at this realisation shows we are beginning to awaken to an aspect of our reality not previously fully acknowledged. When such a discovery is nudged to the front and centre of our awareness, it can leave us disturbed. We are likely to go through a rough period of adjustment but, if put into perspective, it is ultimately for the best that we awaken rather than go on being deluded. The suffering has always been there and our attention was misdirected all along. Now we've come face to face with the true cause of those subtle nagging doubts about our mortal human predicament. But outside a traditional setting—especially in Western culture where you're expected to return to the usual routine of your life without significant change—these adverse reactions can manifest negatively as anything from general discontent to mental turmoil.

I recall well my first retreat and the magnificent insights gained there. I came out extremely enthusiastic about the practice and felt driven to go on to do more and longer retreats. But within months, the awareness set in that I could no longer find delight in the sensory pleasures that used to punctuate my daily existence. Furthermore, previous goals, interests, habits, values, ideals, even friendships, seemed out of place and ill-fitting, a distraction from something more important. I focused on reading about and practising meditation, and talked too much about it with anyone who would listen. Fortunately for others, I was in silent retreat a lot of the time. Then one day I heard a podcast in which two meditation teachers discussed the Dark Night. I was shocked to discover it mapped neatly onto my experience. Hearing their advice that the only way out was to push on, I committed to that, but with a new awareness of the struggles that were actually driving me. For one thing, I tried not to talk about meditation outside meditation circles.

Now let me put on my football coach voice and offer some tough love advice. If these potential downsides sound so awful as to be avoided at all costs, then please forget about meditation retreats, pick up your device, and start scrolling through the latest juicy posts on your favourite social media app. The fact is there for us to discover that our lives are typically lived in a dream-like, unawakened, unwise state. And if meditation works for us at all, it will help snap us out of this enslaved stupor. For many of us, it won't be a pleasant change to go through but, on the upside, it can open up new vistas of knowing ourselves and others. It all comes down to acknowledging what you really want. To know or not to know. To be or not to be. Socrates was quoted as saying the unexamined life is not worth living. He never said the examined life would be an easy ride.

If you are reading this after a retreat and find that the experience has left you in a moody void, you have probably covered enough territory that you're now languishing in the Dark Night. It's a strange congratulations that I offer you. Despite the dark moods, you really have come a long way: further than most people will ever go towards seeing through the illusion they spend their lives entangled in. The good news is that some of the higher stages on the meditation journey can take us to where we finally taste the possibility of release from the torment of the desire-aversion tug-of-war that has dominated our psychological experience until now. After that point, your outlook will take a turn for the better just knowing there is a light at the end of the tunnel.

So if you think you're in your own Dark Night, I can only urge you to push on until you find your way out the other side. If you dive into meditation with energy and determination, it's likely to come up at some stage. If you push on, it will pass. This topic, for all the angst and argumentation around it, really is as simple as that. I will leave you with the encouragement that the good stuff lies on the other side and makes it all worthwhile, so just keep going!

FURTHER RESOURCES

These resources are collected here for inspiration and further detail on meditation matters. The list is far from comprehensive and is only an overview of the vast range of material out there. May you find these helpful.

General meditation

Joseph Goldstein, *Mindfulness: A Practical Guide to Awakening* (Boulder, CO: Sounds True, 2016).
Bhikkhu Ñanamoli, *The Middle Length Discourses of the Buddha: A Translation of the Majjhima Nikaya* (Boston, MA: Wisdom Publications, 1995).
Chogyam Trungpa, *Cutting Through Spiritual Materialism* (Boulder, CO: Shambhala, 2002).
Ajahn Brahm, *Mindfulness, Bliss, and Beyond: A Meditator's Handbook* (Boston, MA: Wisdom Publications, 2006).
Shaila Catherine, *Focused and Fearless: A Meditator's Guide to States of Deep Joy, Calm, and Clarity* (Boston, MA: Wisdom Publications, 2008).

Daily practice & faith

Bhante Gunaratana, *Mindfulness in Plain English* (Boston, MA: Wisdom Publications, 2011).
Ajahn Brahm, *Mindfulness, Bliss, and Beyond: A Meditator's Handbook* (Boston, MA: Wisdom Publications, 2006).
Bhikkhu Ñanamoli, *The Middle Length Discourses of the Buddha: A Translation of the Majjhima Nikaya* (Boston, MA: Wisdom Publications, 1995).
Bhikkhu Bodhi, *The Noble Eightfold Path: Way to the End of Suffering* (Onalaska, WA: BPS Pariyatti, 2020).
Nyanaponika Thera, *Great Disciples of the Buddha: Their Lives, Their Works, Their Legacy* (Boston, MA: Wisdom Publications, 2003).
Bhikkhu Ñanamoli, *The Life of the Buddha: According to the Pali Canon* (Onalaska, WA: Pariyatti Press, 2021).

Enlightenment

Mahasi Sayadaw, *Practical Insight Meditation: Basic and Progressive Stages*, (Kandy: Buddhist Publication Society, 1991). This is an extract from the comprehensive work: Mahasi Sayadaw, *Manual of Insight* (Boston, MA: Wisdom Publications, 2016).
Pa-Auk Tawya Sayadaw, *Knowing and Seeing (Fifth Revised Edition)* (Independently published, 2019).
Sayadaw U Pandita, *In This Very Life: Liberation teachings of the Buddha* (Boston, MA: Wisdom Publications, 2012).
Bhadantacariya Buddhaghosa, *The Path of Purification: The Visuddhimagga* (Onalaska, WA: BPS Pariyatti, 2003).
Jack Kornfield, *A Path with Heart: A Guide through the Perils and Promises of Spiritual Life* (New York: Bantam, 1993).
Jack Kornfield, *After the Ecstasy, the Laundry: How the Heart Grows Wise on the Spiritual Path* (New York: Bantam, 2001).
Daniel M Ingram, *Mastering the Core Teachings of the Buddha: An Unusually Hardcore Dharma Book—Revised and Expanded Edition* (London: Aeon Books, 2018).

Illusory perceptions

Jan Westerhoff, *Twelve Examples of Illusion* (Oxford: Oxford University Press, 2010).
Donald D Hoffman, *The Case Against Reality: How Evolution Hid the Truth From Our Eyes* (London: Penguin, 2020).

Iain McGilchrist, *The Master and His Emissary: The Divided Brain and the Making of the Western World* (New Haven, CT: Yale University Press, 2019).

Metta

Bhante Gunaratana, *Loving-Kindness in Plain English: The Practice of Metta* (Boston, MA: Wisdom Publications, 2017).

Morality

Bhikkhu Bodhi, *The Noble Eightfold Path: Way to the End of Suffering* (Onalaska, WA: BPS Pariyatti, 2020).

On retreat

(Reading on retreat is strongly advised against, but on a long retreat of some months, it does not hurt to bring a text for occasional inspirational reading.)

Acharya Buddharakkhita, *The Dhammapāda: The Buddha's Path of Wisdom* (Onalaska, WA: BPS Pariyatti, 2019).

Bhikkhu Bodhi, *The Noble Eightfold Path: Way to the End of Suffering* (Onalaska, WA: BPS Pariyatti, 2020).

Nyanaponika Thera, *Great Disciples of the Buddha: Their Lives, Their Works, Their Legacy* (Boston, MA: Wisdom Publications, 2003).

Pali materials

Bhante Gunaratana, *Buddhist Suttas for Recitation: A Companion for Walking the Buddha's Path* (Boston, MA: Wisdom Publications, 2019).

Sutta Central, https://suttacentral.net, online library of Pali suttas available in various languages and translations.

Pali-English Online Dictionary, https://dsal.uchicago.edu/dictionaries/pali/, provided by the Pali Text Society.

Introduction to Pali Course, https://learning.pariyatti.org/course/view.php?id=3, provided by the Pariyatti Society.

Samatha and Vipassana

Bhikkhu Sujato, *A Swift Pair of Messengers: Calm with Insight in the Buddha's Words* (Sydney, Australia: Santipada, 2012).

Science

Daniel Goleman, Richard J Davidson, *The Science of Meditation: How to Change Your Brain, Mind and Body* (London: Penguin, 2018). Alternative title: *Altered Traits: Science Reveals How Meditation Changes Your Mind, Brain, and Body.*

Rick Hanson, *Buddha's Brain: The Practical Neuroscience of Happiness, Love, and Wisdom* (Oakland, CA: New Harbinger Publications, 2009).

Web content, podcasts, videos, forums

Deconstructing Yourself Podcast
Guru Viking Podcast
Buddha at the Gas Pump Podcast
Ajahn Brahm Podcast
Access to Insight, https://accesstoinsight.org/, Buddhism resources provided by the Barre Center for Buddhist Studies.
Dharma Overground, https://dharmaoverground.org/, public meditation forum provided by Daniel M Ingram.
Awake Network, https://awakenetwork.org/, members-only meditation forum.
Interviews or talks by or featuring: Bhikkhu Bodhi, Ajahn Brahm, Shaila Catherine, Joseph Goldstein, Bhante Gunaratana, Daniel Ingram, Jack Kornfield, Sharon Salzberg, Michael Taft.

ABOUT THE AUTHOR

Peter Stuckings comes from Australia and has lived around Asia for most of his life due to a fascination with the region's ancient wisdom traditions. He obtained a Masters Degree in Buddhist Studies from Hong Kong University, and also completed Pali language studies in Sri Lanka and with Oxford University. To make the most of the region's training opportunities, he spent some years hopping from country to country and monastery to monastery, which was the inspiration for this book. Nowadays he has taken the robes and dwells as a monk in the forests of Sri Lanka. His blog, called *Places To Meditate*, lists meditation centres of good standing throughout the region.

INDEX

aches and pains, 117
    agitated mind, 118
    coping with uncomfortable mental states, 119
    mental discomfort, 118–119
    mental suffering, 120
agitated mind, 118
Ānāpāna, 182
Ānāpānasati, 59. *See also* concentration meditation instructions
anicca, 143
    examples, 144
    physical experience, 144–146
    sensory experience, 146–147
    Three Marks of Existence, 143
attainments, 193–194. *See also* Enlightenment
aversion (*Vyāpāda*), 166–167. *See also* Five Hindrances

bias, confirmation, 196
bodhi, 188

Buddha, 188, 194–195. *See also* Enlightenment
Buddhism, xiii, 177
    Buddhist strands, xiii
    contact with community, xv–xvi
    Enlightenment, xxi
    Mahayana, xiii
    meals, 11–13
    meditation retreat, 79
    practice of retreating, xv
    six senses, 139
    Theravada, xiii
    Tibetan (or Vajrayana), xiii
    Vassa, xv
Buddhist Enlightenment, 189. *See also* Enlightenment
Buddhist meditation, xxi, 183
    anicca, 143–147
    conceit, 183–186
    effort in meditation, 161–163
    Enlightenment, 187–196
    faith, 177–179
    Five Hindrances, 165–169

goal of Buddhist practice, 196
maps, 171–176
meditation hall, 149–150
training, 177
walking meditation, 157–158
Buddhist strands, xiii
Burmese position, 129. *See also* postures

chair, 131–132. *See also* postures
clothing issue, 16. *See also* retreat
commitment vs. quitting, 69–72.
    See also retreat
community, contact with, xv–xvi
conceit, 183–186
concentration, 181–182. *See also* retreat
    meditation instructions, 59–61
    -related training, 90
confirmation bias, 196
contact with community, xv–xvi
continuity of practice, 89–92. *See also* retreat
Counter-Transference, 87
cross-legged posture, 129–130. *See also* postures
cultural differences, 77. *See also* retreat
    Asian Buddhists vs. Western meditators, 77–78
    Buddhist meditation, 82–83
    expected behaviour towards teacher, 80
    family religious heritage of meditators, 81
    "kowtowing" gesture, 79
    reverential practices towards the Buddha, 79
    segregation by sex, 78
    spiritual friendship, 81–82

daily practice post-retreat, 153–155
    resources, 204
dāna, 45
Dark Night, 197–201
day on retreat, 53–57. *See also* retreat
desire (*Kāmacchanda*), 166–167. *See also* Five Hindrances

Dhamma Hall. *See* meditation hall
Dhamma Talks, 149
dhyāna, xiv
digital device usage, 73–75. *See also* retreat
discomforts and inconveniences, 35–39. *See also* retreat
disruptive scenarios, 66. *See also* retreat
dissatisfaction, instinct for, 99
donations, 45–57. *See also* retreat
dōno, 45
dry Vipassana, 135
dukkha, 198

effort in meditation, 161–163
Eight Precepts, 24, 26–27
Enlightenment, xxi, 134, 187
    Buddha, 194–195
    Buddhist Enlightenment, 189
    claims to attainments, 193–194
    conception of, 188
    European Enlightenment, 188
    Identity View, 190
    illusion of the sense of self, 191
    Pragmatic Dharma, 194
    resources, 204
    sceptics, 195
    sense of self experience, 191–192
    Ten-Fetter Model, 189–190
European Enlightenment, 188. *See also* Enlightenment
exercising, 151–152
Existence, Three Marks of, 143
experience
    physical, 144–146
    sensory, 146–147

faith, 177
    lack of confidence in abilities, 179
    resources, 204
    Sceptical Doubt, 178
Fear Of Missing Out (FOMO), 74
Five Hindrances, 165
    aversion (*Vyāpāda*), 166–167
    desire (*Kāmacchanda*), 166–167

INDEX

restlessness and worry (*uddhacca-kukkucca*), 168
Sceptical Doubt (*Vicikicchā*), 168–169
sloth and torpor (*thīna-middha*), 167
Five Precepts, 24, 25, 26
FOMO. *See* Fear Of Missing Out
full lotus postures, 127. *See also* postures

guru expectations, 87–88

half lotus postures, 128. *See also* postures

Identity View, 190. *See also* Enlightenment
illusion, reality and, xxi
illusory perceptions, 97–98, 204–205
insight meditation instructions, 107–109
intensive meditation training, xi

journaling, 19–21. *See also* retreat

Kāmacchanda. See desire
kneeling. *See also* postures
    with bench, 130–131
    with cushion, 130

Lion posture, 125
Lotus posture, 126
lying down, 125. *See also* postures

Mahasi
    meditation centres, 30–31
    method, 135
    Sayadaw, 135
Mahayana, xiii
maps, 171
    excessive wisdom, 171
    sensory and cognitive experiences, 174–175
    for the territory, 173–174

MBSR (Mindfulness-Based Stress Reduction), 91
meals, 11–13. *See also* retreat
meditation, xi–xii. *See also* retreat
    beginner's mind, xiii
    benefits, xii
    Buddhist, xxi
    equipment, 3–5, 149
    hall, 149–150
    long-term practice, xiv
    methods, xiv
    mind training, xix–xx
    path of intensive, xi
    practice of retreating, xv
    reality and illusion, xxi
    resources, 203
    Samatha, xiv
    Vajrayana/Tantra, xiv
    Vipassana, xiv
    Zen, xiv
meditation centre, 29
    lack of responsiveness from, 31–32
    Mahasi, 30–31
    naming conventions, 31
    residential monastery, 30
    Sri Lankan forest monastery, 31
    types of, 29–30
meditators, 101–103
mental health, 95. *See also* retreat
    dissatisfaction, 99
    meditation as treatment, 96
    psychological struggles, 95
    reality perception break down, 97–98
Metta (loving-kindness) meditation, 102–103
    resources, 205
Middle Way, 134
mind
    agitated, 118
    training, xix–xx
mindfulness, 181–182
Mindfulness-Based Stress Reduction. *See* MBSR

monastery, 30
morality, 113–116
    resources, 205

nīvaraṇa, 166. *See also* Five Hindrances
Noble Silence, 7–10

ordination on retreat, 41
    benefits, 41–42, 44
    piṇḍapāta, 42–43
    Saṅgha, 41
    stipulations, 41

Pa-Auk Sayadaw, 135
pains. *See* aches and pains
Pali, 23
    basic Five Precepts, 24, 25, 26
    chanting, 24
    Eight Precepts, 24, 26–27
    homage to Buddha, 25
    pronunciation, 25
    resources, 205
    Triple Gem, 24, 25
perceptions, illusory,
    97–98, 204–205
piṇḍapāta, 42–43
post-retreat, daily practice,
    153–155
    resources, 204
postures, 123
    Burmese position, 129
    chair, 131–132
    cross-legged, 129–130
    full lotus, 127
    half lotus, 128
    kneeling with bench, 130–131
    kneeling with cushion, 130
    Lion Posture, 125
    Lotus posture, 126
    lying down, 125
    quarter lotus, 128
    sitting, 124–125
    standing, 124
    walking, 123–124
practice continuity, 89–92.
    See also retreat

Pragmatic Dharma, 194. *See also*
    Enlightenment
Precepts
    Eight, 24, 26–27
    Five, 24, 25, 26
preparing yourself, 65–67. *See also*
    retreat

quarter lotus postures, 128. *See also*
    postures

reality and illusion, xxi
restlessness and worry (*uddhacca-
    kukkucca*), 168. *See also*
    Five Hindrances
retreat, xvii–xviii, 13
    challenges, 70
    commitment vs. quitting, 69–72
    concentration meditation
        instructions, 59–61
    concentration-related
        training, 90
    cultural differences, 77–83
    day on retreat, 53–57
    digital device usage, 73–75
    discomforts and
        inconveniences, 35–39
    disruptive scenarios, 66
    donations, 45–57
    issue of clothing, 16
    journaling, 19–21
    leaving retreat, 105–106
    meals, 11–13
    meditation, 79
    at meditation centre, 29–33
    meditation equipment, 3–5
    meditators, 101–103
    mental health, 95–100
    must have list, 17
    Noble Silence, 7–10
    ordination on retreat,
        41–44
    Pali chanting and
        formalities, 23–27
    practice continuity, 89–92
    preparing yourself, 65–67

resources, 205
retreating practice, xv
sleep time, 93–94
teachers, 85–88
things to bring or
    not to bring, 15–18
visas and international
    travel, 49–51

saddhā, 177. *See* faith
Samatha, xiv, 133–137, 181
    resources, 205
Saṅgha, 41
Sceptical Doubt (*Vicikicchā*),
    168–169, 178. *See also* Five
    Hindrances
sense of self, 191–192. *See also*
    Enlightenment
senses, restraint of, 139–141
sensual, 140
sitting, 124–125. *See also* postures
    options, 125–132
six senses, 139
sleep time, 93–94. *See also* retreat
sloth and torpor (*thīna-middha*),
    167. *See also* Five
    Hindrances
sound-proofed room, xviii
standing, 124. *See also* postures

Tantra, xiv
teachers, 85. *See also* retreat
    achievements, 86
    Counter-Transference, 87
    guru expectations, 87–88
    Theravada traditions, 85

Transference, 86–87
Zen, 85, 88
Ten-Fetter Model, 189–190. *See also*
    Enlightenment
Theravada, xiii
thīna-middha. *See* sloth and torpor
things to bring or not, 15–18. *See also*
    retreat
Three Marks of Existence, 143
Tibetan (or Vajrayana), xiii
traditional Buddhist training
    environment, 178
Transference, 86–87

uddhacca-kukkucca. *See*
    restlessness and worry
uncomfortable mental states, 119

Vajrayana/Tantra, xiii, xiv
Vassa, xv
veganism, 12
Vicikicchā. *See* Sceptical Doubt
Vipassana, xiv, 133–137, 181
    resources, 205
virility, 161
visas, 49–51. *See also* retreat
Visuddhimagga, 135
Vyāpāda. *See* aversion

walking, 123–124. *See also* postures
    meditation instructions,
    157–158

yoga, 151

Zen, xiv

www.ingramcontent.com/pod-product-compliance
Lightning Source LLC
Chambersburg PA
CBHW071002160426
43193CB00012B/1879